Elena Quiroga

TWAS 459

Elena Quiroga

ELENA QUIROGA

By PHYLLIS ZATLIN BORING

Rutgers University

TWAYNE PUBLISHERS

A DIVISION OF G. K. HALL & CO., BOSTON

Library of Congress Cataloging in Publication Data

Boring, Phyllis Zatlin.
  Elena Quiroga.

  (Twayne's world authors series; TWAS 459: Spain)
  Bibliography: p. 143–47.
  Includes index.
  1. Quiroga, Elena—Criticism and interpretation.
PQ6631.U57Z6   863'.6'4   77–5953
ISBN 0-8057-6296-5

Contents

About the Author

Phyllis Zatlin Boring holds the A.B. in Spanish and French from Rollins College (Winter Park, Florida) and the M.A. and Ph.D. in Romance Languages from the University of Florida. She presently is Associate Professor of Spanish and Portuguese and Associate Dean at Rutgers College of Rutgers University (New Jersey). Her primary scholarly interest is the contemporary Spanish novel and theater, and she has published articles in various journals including *Romance Notes, Modern Drama, Kentucky Romance Quarterly, Papers on Language & Literature,* and *CLA Journal.* She is co-author of an intermediate level Spanish textbook *Lengua y lectura,* and editor of a college edition of Francisco Ayala's novel *El rapto.*

Preface

With the appearance in 1942 of Camilo José Cela's *La familia de Pascual Duarte (The Family of Pascual Duarte),* the Spanish novel emerged from the ashes of the Civil War and began a period of re-birth. In the decade to follow, a number of young novelists initiated their literary careers and established themselves as major figures in the development of the postwar novel. Among the most important writers in this generation are Cela (1916–), José María Gironella (1917–), Miguel Delibes (1920–), Carment Laforet (1921–), Elena Quiroga (1921–), and Ana María Matute (1926–).

Although there is little question that Elena Quiroga's name should be included in any list of the ten or twelve most important novelists to appear in Spain in the postwar period, her works are little known in the United States and have received, until recently, far less critical attention than that of the other novelists cited. Some of her works are available in French, German, Finnish, and Ukrainian, but no English translation exists of any of her novels. No book-length study of her works is yet in print in any language, and scholarly articles on aspects of her work are very limited in number in both Spanish and English. This lack of secondary sources is difficult to justify in view of the fact that Quiroga won the Nadal Prize for 1950 and the prestigious Premio de la Crítica (Critics' Prize) for 1960, and was chosen as Spain's entrant in the international Rómulo Gallegos novel contest in 1967. There are three explanations for the relative critical neglect of her works. The novel with which Quiroga won the Nadal Prize was considered by many to be a carryover from nineteenth-century Naturalism; the novelist thus was labeled anachronistic, and some critics failed to look at her later works carefully. In the following decade, when Quiroga published the majority of her novels, the dominant current in Spanish literature was social realism. Quiroga, however, was more interested in probing the inner world of her characters and accordingly experimented with a series of innovative narrative tech-niques — interior monologue, stream of consciousness, multiple perspectives, simultaneous time — which were ahead of the times for Spain and therefore neither understood nor appreciated by the general reading public or even by many literary critics. And finally Quiroga has led a quiet life, preferring to remain isolated from literary groups; her desire to avoid publicity has kept her out of the limelight and has made her less visible than other novelists who have become public figures.

In the past several years, however, Quiroga has begun to receive more of the kind of critical attention that her novels deserve. By 1975 her work was the subject of seventeen doctoral dissertations and master's theses completed or in progress in the United States, Spain, and France. After her nomination for the Rómulo Gallegos Prize she also became the object of increasing numbers of interviews by Spanish periodicals. Quite obviously, the years of comparative obscurity are now over and the need for a general study of her works is apparent.

In the preparation of the current book I was fortunate in having the full and generous cooperation of Elena Quiroga. Little accurate biographical data on the author had been available in the past, and she graciously supplied me with this information. In interviews and correspondence she also shared with me her own opinions on the novel in general, and on some of her works in particular. She was especially helpful in clarifying for me her intentions in writing certain novels and in outlining for me the novel she was working on at the time of this writing. Moreover, she lent me a large collection of book reviews and interviews from Spanish and Latin American periodicals that would otherwise have been difficult to locate. In the notes and bibliography I have emphasized the secondary sources that are most readily available to students and scholars in the United States, but I have also benefited from the materials in the author's collection and from other articles I was able to study at libraries in Madrid.

Quiroga's novel is multifaceted, and I have therefore not limited the present study to any one critical approach to her literature but have rather attempted to analyze various aspects of each of her works, with emphasis on her development as a psychological novelist, her use of structural and narrative techniques, and her view of Spanish society. The initial chapter of the book is a general introduction to the author's life and work. The next five chapters include individual studies of each of her novels and novelettes, with indications of how these works relate to one another and to other works of Spanish and world literature. The final chapter is an overview of several dominant tendencies and themes found throughout her novelistic production.

I am very much indebted to Elena Quiroga for her help with my research. Without her cooperation it would have been impossible to obtain much important information, particularly the biographical data. I would like to express my appreciation both to her and to her husband, Dalmiro de la Válgoma, for their kindness in receiving me and my children in their home and for patiently answering my many questions. I would also like to thank Professor Janet Winecoff Díaz for her helpful advice and encouragement throughout this project and to Doris Caruso for her careful and thoughtful assistance in the preparation of the manuscript.

PHYLLIS ZATLIN BORING

Rutgers University

Chronology

1921 Elena Quiroga born in the province of Santander, Spain.

1922 Mother dies.

1930 Becomes boarding student at Catholic girls' school on the outskirts of Bilbao.

1931 King Alfonso XIII leaves the Spanish throne. Beginning of the Second Republic.

1936 June, leaves the boarding school in Bilbao; goes to Rome to complete her high school education. July, outbreak of the Spanish Civil War.

1938 Returns to Spain after visiting southern France. Spends the remainder of the war years in Villoria.

1939 Civil War ends.

1941 Spends this winter and the following one in Barcelona.

1942 Moves with father to La Coruña.

1949 Publishes *La soledad sonora (Sonorous Solitude)*.

1950 Marries the historian Dalmiro de la Válgoma. Moves to Madrid.

1951 January 6, awarded the Nadal Prize for *Viento del norte (Northwind)*.

1952 Publishes *La sangre (Blood)*.

1953 Two novelettes, *La otra ciudad (The Other City)* and *Trayecto uno (Bus One)*, appear in the series "La Novela del Sábado." Father dies.

1954 *Algo pasa en la calle (Something's Happening in the Street)*.

1955 April, *La enferma (The Sick Woman)*; December, *La careta (The Mask)*.

1956 *Plácida, la joven (The Young Plácida)*.

1958 *La última corrida (The Last Bullfight)*.

1960 *Tristura (Sadness)*, which wins the Premio de la Crítica (Critics' Prize).

1965 *Escribo tu nombre (I Write Your Name)*.

1967 *I Write Your Name* is chosen to represent Spain in the first international contest for the Rómulo Gallegos Novel Prize.

1968   Husband is named permanent librarian and permanent secretary of the Royal Academy of History. Moves from the Calle de Ferraz to the Royal Academy of History building on the Calle de León.

1973   *Presente profundo (Profound Present).*

1976   At work on *Se acabó todo, muchacha triste (It's All Over Now, Baby Blue).*

CHAPTER 1

Elena Quiroga: Solitary Novelist

I Childhood and Adolescence

E LENA Quiroga was born October 26, 1921, in the province of Santander, the sixteenth child in a family of seventeen children. Her father, José Quiroga Velarde, was a landowner from Galicia whose family's ancestral home was located in Villoria in the province of Orense. Of a noble family, he held the title of Conde de San Martín de Quiroga, but Quiroga herself rejects the family's nobility as being of no importance.[1] Quiroga's mother, Isabel Abarca Fornés, was from Santander and preferred to return there for the birth of her children.[2] It was for this reason that Quiroga, who frequently shows her love of Galicia in her writings, was born in the northern coastal city.

Of her mother Quiroga knows very little, for Isabel Abarca died when Elena was not yet two years old and her younger sister was still an infant. The absence of a mother undoubtedly made a strong impression on the future novelist, for many of Quiroga's characters are orphans, and she frequently treats with great sensitivity the isolation of the person who feels unloved.

Quiroga spent her childhood with her father and her brothers and sisters in Villoria. When she was only five or six, she and her little sister were asked to decide whether they wished to remain in Galicia with their father or go to Santander to be raised by their maternal grandmother. In retrospect, Quiroga now wonders how such an important decision could have been required of such small children. Elena chose to stay, but the younger child and their oldest sister went to Santander. In Quiroga's first novel *La soledad sonora (Sonorous Solitude)* and in her later novels about Tadea — *Tristura (Sadness)* and *Escribo tu nombre (I Write Your Name)* — she narrates the experiences of a little girl who is separated from her father and her brothers and raised among relatives who show her little if

13

any affection. While these novels undoubtedly relate somewhat to
the writer's own childhood, she has obviously not modeled them
completely on her own experiences.

Quiroga does, in fact, recall aspects of her childhood with great
warmth. She enjoyed the freedom of living in the countryside: "I
loved the wild and independent life that my father and I had in the
village." Her love of nature and animals, developed as a child, is
frequently reflected in her novels. Quiroga also notes that having
come from such a large family, she had the advantage of a "school
of life" without ever leaving the house; she has since drawn upon
their lives and experiences as inspiration for some of her novelistic
characters and situations. With so many brothers and sisters, the
family referred to the children in terms of groups: the big ones, the
middle-sized ones, and the little ones. As Elena herself was one of
the little ones, the oldest children were almost grown by the time
she was born. She has credited the older children with helping her
to mature her narrative style before beginning to write, for they
laughed at her early efforts to tell stories, thus forcing her to set
higher standards for herself.[3]

Quiroga learned to love reading as a young chlild and while in
her father's home became acquainted with the great works of literature. She had access to her paternal grandfather's library, which
she categorizes as Voltairian. She points out that her situation was
exceptional in Spain in the 1920s and 1930s, for at that time many
Spaniards considered books other than religious ones to be improper for women and children. "In Spain, you had to hide to
read," she recalls. Among Elena's favorite authors was her fellow
Galician, Ramón María del Valle-Inclán. Once when the young girl
was visiting at her grandmother's house in Santander she offered a
commentary on Valle-Inclán. Her mother's family was horrified
that the child had read such books, and she was equally astonished
that they had not. On another occasion a maternal aunt cautioned
her not to speak of *Crime and Punishment* in front of her children.

Although Quiroga herself fortunately had the opportunity to
read and develop her interest in literature, in her novels she often
shows the repressive attitude typical of the period. She does so
briefly in *Sonorous Solitude* and the short novel *Trayecto uno (Bus
One)* and more extensively in *Sadness* and *I Write Your Name.*
Quiroga found that the latter novels must have captured the reality
of prewar Spain, for she received an astonishing number of letters

from people who identified the atmosphere she described with the one they had experienced as children. In her view, it is not important whether what the child reads is "good" or "bad" but whether the child is.

Although grateful for the freedom her father gave her, the novelist remembers her father as being a very proper and formal man who did not outwardly show affection or tenderness toward his children. Perhaps it was for this reason that the young Elena often sought out the companionship of the servants in the warmth of the kitchen.[4] The hours spent there are reflected in her novels in at least two respects. She describes the world of the servants with great sympathy and authenticity in such works as *Viento del norte (Northwind)* and *I Write Your Name,* and the stories she heard there of Galician life became sources of inspiration for some of her later creative works. She remembers having been very impressed as a child by tales of women who killed their husbands by giving them small doses of poison over an extended period of time; when Dolores in *La sangre (Blood)* attempts to murder her husband by this means, Quiroga is drawing on the kitchen talk of her childhood.

At the age of nine Elena was sent off to a boarding school on the outskirts of Bilbao. As was typical for Spain, the school was for girls only and was run by Catholic nuns. The rigidity of such a school must have come as quite a shock to a child who had been free to roam the countryside near her father's home and to read whatever interested her. Like her character Tadea, Elena did not adjust to the school and ultimately decided to leave and not return. During her five years of boarding school, Elena often spent her Christmas and Easter vacations at her grandmother's home in Santander. Apart from the obvious reason that Santander was much closer to Bilbao than was Villoria, Quiroga's father wanted her to have the opportunity to know her mother's family.

By 1936 Elena had determined that she could no longer tolerate the atmosphere of her boarding school. For a while her father considered sending her to England to finish her education, but because of the uncertain political situation in Spain, he finally chose Rome instead. Quiroga considers the period she spent in Rome to have been of utmost importance in shaping her future career as a novelist. She attended a boarding school there specializing in arts and humanities, but of greater meaning for her than the school was the city itself: "I believe that Rome gave me a sense of harmony. Rome is a revelation for anyone who has a creative or artistic instinct." She recalls that for someone coming from puritanical Spain, Rome was like an explosion of sensuality, beauty of form, and musicality. When the Spanish Civil War began in July, 1936, Quiroga was still in Rome. At Christmas vacation in 1937 she returned to Spain, stopping to sightsee in southern France. To date this trip to Italy and France has been her only travel experience outside her native country.

Arriving in Spain in early 1938, Quiroga went to her father's home in Villoria. The little village in Galicia was far removed from the front lines, and the news of the Civil War reached them there only indirectly. Nevertheless, the novelist recalls that the people were deeply affected by the civil strife. In the novel she is currently writing, *Se acabó todo, muchacha triste (It's All Over Now, Baby Blue)* the third in the Tadea series, she relates the impact of the war on the sensitivities of those in such an isolated place.

II *Adulthood*

For the remainder of the Spanish Civil War, which ended in 1939, and the years immediately following, Quiroga lived in the relative tranquillity of the Galician village. By this time her formal education was over. She has pointed out on occasion that when she was growing up many Spaniards still considered a university education to be quite improper for a woman in particular and probably sinful for anyone.[5] Her father, however, did not share this opinion and would have supported her in her desire to study philosophy and letters had he been able to do so financially. But, by the time Elena was ready for college, he had already been forced to sell parcels of his property to help the older children establish themselves, and she did not want to force upon him further sacrifices. Her love of books had not diminished, and she continued to read on her own. She considers herself largely self-taught and believes that in the 1940s she had a firsthand knowledge of foreign writers that few other Spanish novelists of the day could claim.

The winters of 1941 and 1942 were spent in Barcelona, where Quiroga went to care for the little daughter of her widowed older brother. Also in 1942 Quiroga's father moved to La Coruña, one of the four provincial capitals of the region of Galicia and a busy port city on the Atlantic coast. In La Coruña the young woman spent many hours reading in the library and was surprised to find herself often alone there. She developed a disdain for the middle class who took no interest in books and learning; others, in turn, viewed her studious traits in amazement and predicted that she would never marry. Unconcerned, Quiroga continued to read and to walk, taking long strolls into the countryside, listening to the people. Eager to absorb more of the region, she supplemented her walks with rides in rickety old buses to visit neighboring villages. Her firsthand knowledge of the Galician countryside and customs was later to form the background of several of her novelistic works. It was in La Coruña that Quiroga began her literary career. Except for one newspaper article, of which even she no longer has a copy, her first published work was *Sonorous Solitude.* Printing of this novel, the writing of which was completed in 1948, was sponsored by the Provincial Diputation of La Coruña. *Sonorous Solitude* did not attract a great deal of attraction and, as is often the case with first novels, is decidedly inferior to the author's later works. Quiroga herself no longer considers the book important and views it merely as a first try.[6] Her second novel, *Northwind,* however, won the prestigious Nadal Prize for 1950 and established the young writer as one of the important new novelists of Spain's postwar era.

The decade to follow was one of intense literary activity, with the publication of six major novels and three novelettes in rapid succession: *La Sangre (Blood),* 1952; *La otra ciudad (The Other City)* and *Trayecto uno (Bus One),* 1953; *Algo pasa en la calle (Something's Happening in the Street),* 1954; *La enferma (The Sick Woman)* and *La careta (The Mask),* 1955; *Plácida, la joven (The Young Plácida),* 1956; *La última corrida (The Last Bullfight),* 1958; *Tristura (Sadness),* 1960. While many critics had written negatively of *Northwind* and argued that the work was too "traditional" or close to nineteenth-century narrative technique, it was impossible for them to level the same criticism at the following works. Quiroga's novels of the 1950s were unquestionably innovative, differing not only among themselves but also standing apart from dominant currents in the Spanish novel of the period. They were, in fact, so different that in many cases the critics were unprepared for them and found them too experimental or too difficult to understand. Most other novelists were concentrating on the contemporary reality of Spain, showing the problematic external aspects of society in a theoretically objective manner. Quiroga, however, was more interested in the internal psychological reality of the individual; and she accordingly tended to employ such techniques as interior monologues, stream of consciousness, and multiperspective rather than the impassive narration of social realism. Quiroga's novels of the 1950s are thus characterized by innovations in structure not generally found in the Spanish novel until well into the 1960s. They also tend to be more imaginative and poetic than many other novels written in Spain at the same time.[7]

Ironically, although Quiroga was less interested in social reality than were the majority of her contemporaries, her novels of the 1950s do introduce some socially significant themes not carefully studied by other writers until a decade or more later. *Something's Happening in the Street,* for example, shows the psychological and sociological impact of divorce in Spanish society, a theme not extensively dealt with by others until the end of the 1960s. José Corrales Egea identifies the period from 1965 to 1970 as being the one when Spanish novelists began to demythologize the Spanish Civil War,[8] but Quiroga had already done so in *The Mask* where she skillfully revealed the long-term psychological aftermath of the war. Her novels of this period are noteworthy not only for the constant development of style and form but also for the wide variety of characters, situations, and themes that she presents. Gonzalo Torrente Ballester has commented that of contemporary Galician novelists writing in Spanish, only he and Quiroga treat their native region,[9] and indeed, most of her novels are set entirely or partially in Galicia, but her settings also include Madrid and La Mancha, and her characters range from peasant women to college professors to bullfighters.

Quiroga's novelistic focus naturally separated her from association with any Spanish literary groups, and her personal life-style reinforced this isolation. In 1950, she married the Galician historian and genealogist Dalmiro de la Válgoma. They moved to Madrid to an apartment on Calle de Ferraz in the Argüelles section of the city. Although Quiroga's marriage in no way detracted from her intensive literary production, she took pride in her home and relished the privacy of her family life. Shunning publicity, she became known as the writer least seen in public and least likely to be the subject of interviews.[10] For this reason few references to her life appear in critical writings about her works, and what little information is given is often erroneous, possibly based on speculation. The author assumes that this explains why her birthdate is inaccurate in many sources, and she has assured the present writer that she would have been happy to clarify some of these biographical questions had anyone ever asked her.

Quiroga's thorough familiarity with the Spanish capital is apparent in the works in which Madrid is the setting: *Bus One, Something's Happening in the Street,* and part of *The Mask.* She always describes the backgrounds of her narratives with great authenticity, based on firsthand knowledge. To prepare for *The Last Bullfight,* which takes place in La Mancha, she spent several months in the region to absorb the atmosphere. Frequently also she has left Madrid to find the necessary peace and quiet for her creative work. Sometimes she has lived briefly in the homes of friends or relatives in the provinces, but more typically she has enjoyed the tranquillity of her husband's family home in Galicia. Located in Nigrán (Pontevedra), the Pazo de Nigrán is a country home located on a deadend road and therefore quite isolated from the outside world. Quiroga describes the old house as "poetic" and speaks of the region with great affection. She and her husband have spent several months annually in this remote spot since the second year of their marriage. Quiroga, who often displays a deep understanding of children in her novels, has no children of her own. However, one of her husband's nephews, now grown, lived with them from the time he was four years old.[11]

Although Quiroga's fiction was outside the mainstream of the Spanish novel of the 1950s and the author herself tried to stay out of the public eye, her importance as a novelist did not go unnoticed. A number of translations of her works have appeared in other European countries, including *Blood* in Finland in 1955 and in France in 1957; *Northwind* in Germany in 1956 and in Belgium in 1963; *The Mask* in France in 1959; *The Sick Woman* in France in 1961; *Something's Happening in the Street* in Germany in 1963; and *Blood* and *I Write Your Name* in Ukrainia. In some respects Quiroga's novels were better received outside Spain than in her own country, for they were more closely related in their narrative and structural techniques to the contemporary European novel in general than to the Spanish novel in particular.

Quiroga's first novel, *Sonorous Solitude,* had drawn in part upon her own experiences, at least in the initial creation of character. For the subsequent novels published in the 1950s, she abandoned the autobiographical tendency. With *Sadness,* however, she returned once again to a child character, Tadea, who has a close relationship with the author. Although Tadea is not strictly an autobiographical figure, Quiroga points out that the character shares much of her own life experiences. The chronology of author and character is almost identical — year of birth, death of mother, reaction to social and political turmoil preceding the Civil War, unhappiness with the Catholic boarding school. *Sadness* was awarded the Premio de la Crítica literary prize for 1960, and the author has subsequently written two more novels dealing with the same character. *I Write Your Name* recounts Tadea's years in boarding school during the years immediately preceding the Civil War, and *It's All Over Now, Baby Blue,* the war years themselves.

From 1960 on, Quiroga diminished the intensive pace that marked her productivity of the previous decade. *I Write Your Name,* her most extensive novel to date, is almost seven hundred pages long and required four years to write. Published in 1965, this novel, like *Sadness* before it, was well received by the critics. Spanish novelists generally were no longer concentrating on social realism, Spanish literary critics had become more sophisticated, and Quiroga herself had evolved in her novelistic art; these combined factors assured the author a more appreciative audience than that of the mid-1950s. In 1967 a committee of the Royal Spanish Academy, consisting of José María de Cossío, Manuel Halcón, and Julián Marías, was asked to choose a novel written in the previous three-year period to represent Spain in the first international competition for the Rómulo Gallegos Prize. Their choice was *I Write Your Name,* and suddenly Quiroga became the subject of nationwide attention. Interviews and stories about her appeared in newspapers and magazines across the country.

In 1968 Quiroga and her husband moved from the Calle de Ferraz, where they had lived since they were first married, to the Royal Academy of History on the Calle de León. Dalmiro de la Válgoma serves as permanent secretary to the Academy, and it is his position that has given the couple the opportunity to live in this magnificent building in one of the older sections of the city. Located in an area of narrow, winding streets, not far from the Puerta del Sol, the well-restored red brick façade bears a commemorative plaque to Marcelino Menéndez y Pelayo, the famous Spanish scholar who for many years served as librarian of the

Academy. Quiroga and her husband live in the same apartment that Menéndez y Pelayo once occupied. The author expresses a deep sense of satisfaction with her home, not only for its historical significance, but also for the relative peace and quiet it affords her. The solid construction of the old palace blocks out much street noise and provides a tranquil environment in the midst of busy Madrid. The library, where she does much of her work, particularly gives this peaceful impression. The ceiling-high bookcases and the various paintings reflect the cultural and literary interests of the couple, and a large model of a ship reminds one of their connection to Galicia and the sea.

Following completion of the monumental *I Write Your Name,* and perhaps exhausted by that effort, Quiroga wrote no novels for several years. In an interview in 1967 she spoke of a projected work about an attempted suicide and two doctors who probed for motives,[12] but that seed of a novel was not to germinate until *Presente profundo (Profound Present)* in 1973. As frequently in her creative process, Quiroga's initial idea for a novel evolved considerably as the work itself progressed. *Profound Present* has one doctor, Rubén, who attempts to probe the motives for two suicides, that of a lower-class, aging woman from rural Galicia and that of a wealthy, cosmopolitan young woman. Structurally the novel is a return to Quiroga's experimental works of the 1950s, for she develops here a counterpoint between the two stories. Also of interest, as indicated by the title, is her treatment of time.

Quiroga in the 1970s may be returning to a more intense productivity than in the preceding period. The third in the Tadea series, *It's All Over Now, Baby Blue,* was begun not long after the publication of *Profound Present,* and when it was only partially written, Quiroga told the present writer of an idea already in mind for her next work. The author was particularly fascinated by a newspaper account of a mother in Italy whose son had disappeared. When this woman learned of an unidentified young man in a coma, she went to the hospital and thought she recognized him, in spite of his facial injuries. For three months she visited him daily. At the end of that time, when the young man was dying, the woman's real son, who had been in hiding from the police, came to her in secret and told her of her mistake. For a few minutes she was overjoyed, but then she turned her back on him, returning to the hospital to maintain her vigil by the side of her dead "son." Quiroga, who has always shown a deep interest in the psychological motivation for apparently inexplicable acts, would like to probe the inner feelings of a mother who would reject the living son in favor of a dead man who presumably should have meant nothing to her. Also possible for future novels is a continuation of the Tadea cycle.[13]

Unlike many contemporary Spanish novelists, who write short stories, newspaper and magazine articles, and literary criticism in addition to their long narrative works, Quiroga has written almost nothing but novels and novelettes. In 1952, at her husband's request, she wrote the prologue to his genealogical study of the nineteenth-century novelist, Countess Emilia Pardo Bazán. She has also authored three little books that the family printed privately for distribution to friends: a short story, "El pájaro de oro" ("The Golden Bird"); "Carta a Cadaqués" ("Letter to Cadaqués"), which is a poem written to friends who had allowed her to use their home on the Costa Brava while working on *Sadness,* describing the view of the sea, the landscape and the people she enjoyed there; and "Envío al Faramello" ("Message to Faramello"), a tribute in photographs and poetry to an old friend in that Galician village.

If at one time Quiroga's works received comparatively little critical attention, that same situation no longer exists. Recently seventeen graduate students in North America and Europe have made her novels the subject of theses they are preparing. Quiroga now finds that she receives so many requests for information that, were she to attempt to answer them, she would have no time left to write. She has no secretarial help and types both rough and finished drafts of her novels herself. Quiroga also notes that, unlike many middle-class Spanish women who have full-time help in the home, she has only a part-time day maid and does much housework and cooking herself. When at work on a novel, she tends to draft a section in the morning which she then rereads and puts in final form in the afternoon, following the long Spanish lunch.[14] She then generally rests in the late afternoon, leaving the early evening hours free for visits with family friends, and enjoys a peaceful late-evening supper with her husband.[15] Her life revolves around her literary work, her home, her family and friends.

III   *Quiroga's Views on Novels and Novelists*

In 1951, when Quiroga first attracted widespread attention for *Northwind,* many critics compared her work to the nineteenth-century novels of Pardo Bazán.[16] Later, however, with the appearance of her more innovative works, she was frequently accused of imitating Faulkner. While Sainz de Robles is probably unique in proclaiming that Quiroga wrote better novels when she followed Pardo Bazán than when she followed Faulkner,[17] many other writers criticized such novels as *Something's Happening in the Street, The Sick Woman,* and *The Mask* as unnecessarily complicated, experimental, or Faulknerian. Always a strong defender of Quiroga's narrative technique, Entrambasaguas has suggested that these critics failed to recognize her exceptional talent and originality.[18]

Looking back at these early reactions to her novels, Quiroga feels that Spanish literary criticism was not as sophisticated then as it is now. She finds little resemblance between her first novels and those that Pardo Bazán wrote sixty years before, but presumes that critics made the parallel simply because both writers were Galician women writing about Galicia. She notes also that because Pardo Bazán's husband's name was Quiroga, many people have erroneously assumed that the two novelists are related,[19] even though Quiroga is a very common name in Galicia. Given these superficial similarities, the critics apparently looked no farther. Quiroga herself admires Pardo Bazán as a writer of short stories but has serious reservations about her novels, particularly with respect to the development of character. She feels that Pardo Bazán manipulates her characters to meet the needs of her plot and that the author's hand is always visible. Moreover, she finds these characters to be unrealistically monolithic: "I believe that no one is so one-sided, all good or all bad. We do not always react the same way; it depends on the day, the circumstances, who is with us."

Quiroga likewise rejects the contention that she consciously imitated Faulkner, although she believes that his influence on the contemporary novel has been so great that it would be impossible for a novelist today to divorce himself completely from Faulknerian techniques: "Today we write after Faulkner, just as we write by electric light, not candlelight." She also notes that contemporary novelists write with twentieth-century verb forms, not seventeenth-century ones, and with twentieth-century narrative techniques, not those of earlier periods. Maurice Coindreau, who prepared French translations of novels by both Faulkner and Quiroga for Gallimard, finds a major difference between the two writers in their concept of time. He says that Faulkner's characters are prisoners of the past, while Quiroga's characters live in a present that merges with past and future.[20] That constitutes, for Quiroga, her concept of "profound present" and is a judgment with which she completely agrees.

The writer with whom Quiroga acknowledges greater kinship than with either Pardo Bazán or Faulkner is Valle-Inclán, whose works she admires as much today as in her childhood. For example, in *Blood,* Quiroga wanted to show the end of a race and the total decadence of a family, a theme clearly handled by Valle-Inclán well before Faulkner.[21] She feels that scholars should not only be studying the influence of Faulkner on her generation of Spanish novelists but also the influence of Valle-Inclán on Faulkner.[22]

But, for Quiroga, a good novelist does not deliberately choose a narrative technique or novelistic structure and then write a novel to fit the mold. Rather she feels that a particular theme will suggest its own appropriate form and that the form and content of a modern novel cannot be separated. In part for this reason she rejects the French *nouveau roman* and the example of Robbe-Grillet as being more scientific than literary. To several interviewers she has mentioned that the actual writing of the novel poses no difficulties for her. After *Northwind* she had acquired enough self-confidence to write with ease.[23] The idea for the novel may be with her for an extended period of time before she begins to put the story on paper. When it has become almost an obsession with her, she then begins to work, but always without notes.[24] In this respect Quiroga is in basic agreement with Miguel de Unamuno and his concept of the novel as a living form and the characters as autonomous beings that take shape on their own: "I believe that an authentic novelist proposes nothing to himself at the moment of writing. The novel creates a world. The author never knows what will emerge."[25] To the present writer Quiroga commented that the completion of *"It's All Over Now, Baby Blue"* would go quickly because the final chapters of a novel tend to write themselves.

Although critics frequently praise Quiroga's style, the author herself feels that style is far less important to a novel than either rhythm or life: "Without rhythm there is no novelist. I believe that style is not necessary. What is important is life, that the novel create a world. . . . I write with real passion. . . . I avoid elaborations. It is the characters who exert pressure on me. Then I become a medium."[26]

Quiroga lives a secluded life, but she does not consider this a disadvantage in terms of novelistic creation. She agrees with Pío Baroja that the novelist ought to be a solitary observer.[27] Her novels are based on reality, for she feels that she could not write about what she does not know, but she then feels that it is the novelist's mission to transform that reality into artistic creation. Rejecting the concept that literature can or should serve as a vehicle of propaganda or denunciation, she nevertheless holds that all novels are essentially social.[28] A novelist must be able to absorb his surroundings.[29] The inspirations for her characters and situations come from composites of people she has known or heard about or from incidents she has read about in the newspapers. She believes that news accounts of accidents and crimes reflect very well the social psychology of a given historic moment. But the literary creation seldom has a direct relationship to any concrete person or situation. Of her many characters, only Plácida and Liberata of *The Sick Woman* are based with little modification on specific people.

In the years following the Spanish Civil War, more women have become important novelists than in all of Spain's previous literary history. Critics have often responded to the phenomenon by questioning what makes the woman novelist different from the man. Although Quiroga concedes that the novelty of being a woman novelist may have been an advantage in the 1950s,[30] personally she sees no reason for making distinctions between male and female writers.[31] For her the important matter to consider is not the sex of the novelist but the novel.[32] Similarly she upholds the right of women in general to equal opportunity in all fields, but she rejects the label of "feminist," feeling that it connotes a belief that the sexes are equal while she sees them as being complementary. Defending the portrayal of feminine characters in her novels, she asserts that she has not looked down on Spanish women,[33] but that Spanish women in general lack depth because they have been denied an adequate education.[34]

In essence, Quiroga has sought in her novels to explore the inner psychology of human beings: "I write from within myself in journeys that go deeper into people, because what is important to me beyond mere existence is man's profound being, to explain it to myself and to explain it to others."[35] For her human experience cuts across social class; everyone shares the same sense of life, a similar

lack of understanding of the people who surround him. Her repeated themes are solitude and the inability of the individual to
communicate his or her deep inner feelings to others. In her works
Quiroga probes the hidden identities of her characters, but because
she does so within the context of a fixed moment in time, she also
gives us the sociological background and hence a realistic view of
prewar and postwar Spain. Given her skillful use of innovative
narrative techniques, Quiroga's novels are thus of great interest on
three levels: psychological, sociological, and structural.

CHAPTER 2

The Early Novels

I Sonorous Solitude

QUIROGA's first novel, *La soledad sonora (Sonorous Solitude),* did not attract much attention upon publication in 1949 and has been out of print for some years. It is an admittedly immature work, and the author prefers to have it forgotten.[1] Despite its defects, however, *Sonorous Solitude* is interesting for its introduction of themes and characters later developed in other works.

The main character, Elisa, has lived with her maternal grandmother since the death of her mother when Elisa was three years old. Her sister Teresa is also raised by the grandmother, but their five older brothers remain with their father, whom they seldom see. The novel is divided into three parts, the first of which gives the adolescent Elisa's memories of her childhood. She had been a lonely, taciturn child, tyrannized by a governess, her aunts, and her cousins. The second part finds Elisa entering womanhood, with the recounting of her first infatuation, her marriage to the youthful Diego just after the Spanish Civil War, their brief honeymoon, his decision to fight with Hitler's forces against the Communists on the Russian front, the news of his death, and Elisa's subsequent love for José, the mature man for whom she had been truly destined. In the third part, Elisa, who had still felt alone even when married to Diego, now is happy at last. She is married to José and they await the birth of their first child. But, thanks to a series of premonitions throughout the novel, the reader is not surprised that they do not live happily ever after. News arrives that Diego is not dead. From the shock Elisa loses the baby and almost dies. Upon her recovery, she determines that she could not respect Diego if he were to take her back nor could she remain with José whom she loves. She de-

cides therefore to live alone in her grandmother's house and raise
her niece, whose mother died in childbirth. Having made this decision at the age of twenty-three she accepts her future life of solitude
and thereby finds peace.

The plot is melodramatic in the extreme, as are the characters.
Although in the portrayal of Elisa there is some indication of
Quiroga's future skill as a psychological novelist, for the most part
the characters here are unrealistic stereotypes. Elisa is so mistreated
by her aunts and cousins that the story begins to resemble *Cinderella*. Indeed, it is at her first ball that a transformed Elisa is suddenly recognized for her beauty and attracts the attention of Diego,
the handsome, wealthy young man her cousins had hoped to marry.
If Diego is "Prince Charming," grandmother may well be the fairy
godmother, in that she had previously rescued Elisa from the
clutches of the evil governess and had provided her with some freedom from the aunts' persecution.

The exaggeration of character sometimes is the result of sexual
stereotyping. Elisa's cousins, in their talk of trapping future husbands, are catty, hypocritical, and deceitful. Pedro, Elisa's first
love, is a Don Juan figure who deliberately plans to seduce his
fifteen-year-old cousin, an effort which she resists although she
does meet him secretly in the garden on several occasions. Elisa,
while supposed to be very different from other women her age,
nevertheless has an overwhelming maternal instinct and frequently
mentions wanting many children; in the spring following Diego's
alleged death, she suffers because "only she was not in bloom.
Only she was sterile" (*S,* 170). The women characters in general are
willingly subservient, allowing the men to decide for them what
they should do during the war years, for example, and admitting
that they do not understand such matters. José is even more ideal-
ized than Diego: "Diego was an archangel. José is a man of flesh
and blood" (*S,* 200). Accordingly, José epitomizes manly strength,
as Elisa notes when she first unburdens her soul to him: "And the
sensation of shelter and protection that enveloped her now,
emanating from that masculine power, took possession of her" (*S,*
181). To reinforce the traditional concept of marriage between the
strong male and the innocent female, we learn that for José Elisa is
still a virgin, in spite of her having been Diego's wife: "Yes, she is a
virgin. Purer, more inexperienced than if she were a maiden" (*S,*
213).

In addition to a disturbing emphasis on fatality and coincidence, the plot of the novel is forced in other ways. For example, Elisa falls ill and almost dies three times. She has typhoid fever just before she meets Diego. After Diego is supposedly dead and she finds herself suffering internal conflict because of her love for José, she looks to the heavens for a sign and sees a shooting star. This so unnerves her that she falls into a delirious state and is ill for weeks. Also, as mentioned before, she almost dies after learning that Diego is alive. The repetition would be upsetting enough if Elisa were depicted as a sickly, unstable person, but on the contrary, she is generally shown to be healthy and able to withstand other emotional pressure.

The flaws in the work are many, but they are ones often found in first novels. Some critics have, in fact, overlooked the defects and found positive values in the novel. Joaquín de Entrambasaguas wrote a glowing review of *Sonorous Solitude* in which he termed Elisa "one of the most interesting feminine characters in the contemporary novel."[2] Similarly, Albert Brent later called *Sonorous Solitude* "a penetrating character study."[3] Valbuena Prat felt that Quiroga's first work was a "fine promise of awakened sensitivity."[4] Entrambasaguas reported that the novel had been recommended for the Nadal Prize, so it did not pass unnoticed on the Spanish literary scene.

Viewing *Sonorous Solitude* from the vantage point of the present, this first novel has its greatest interest as an indication of themes and situations prevalent in more mature works. Elisa and her family are obviously closely related to the characters of the Tadea novels, based to some extent on similar autobiographical elements. A comparison between *Sonorous Solitude* and *Sadness* does, therefore, reveal just how much the author developed her novelistic skills in the intervening years. The romanticism and stylistic defects of *Sonorous Solitude* disappear. In *Sadness* Quiroga writes the entire novel in the early childhood of her character rather than covering those years as only one part of the whole, as in *Sonorous Solitude;* the more intensive treatment in the later work allows her to develop her characters from within rather than merely presenting them externally as she does in *Sonorous Solitude* through an omniscient narrator. She also makes numerous changes in her cast of characters. The unbelievable evil governess of the early novel is replaced by two much more credible figures in

Sadness. In *Sonorous Solitude,* given the closeness of Elisa and her sister Teresa, it is hard to believe that Elisa was so miserably lonely in her childhood. In *Sadness* Quiroga makes the child's solitude more believable by eliminating the sister, and she allows us to witness Tadea's loneliness for ourselves rather than making repeated external references to solitude as in *Sonorous Solitude.* In *Sonorous Solitude,* Quiroga anachronistically interpolates the romance of Elisa's father and mother within the adolescent's memories of childhood; the device is defective, for Elisa would not have known the details of that story nor would they logically belong in her own chronological recounting of her life. In *Sadness,* by contrast, Tadea's knowledge of her mother comes in bits and pieces, gleaned from the conversation of relatives and servants. In both cases the child feels a great sense of loss at having no mother and spends time fantasizing about her and yearning for someone to replace that missing love and affection; the analysis of the psychological impact of this tragedy on Elisa's character is one of the most successful aspects of *Sonorous Solitude.*

Elisa in many respects is a forerunner of a repeated figure in Quiroga's novels, not only because of the obvious relationship with Tadea but also with other characters, both male and female. She is a lonely person who has difficulty communicating her inner feelings to others. For this reason she is accused of having no heart, when in fact she suffers deeply behind the mask of taciturn indifference used to protect herself.[5] Although not all of Quiroga's silent, lonely charcters are orphans like Elisa, most have become alienated due to some special circumstance in their childhoods. Elisa is different from these in that she is able to leave her protective shell for a time and be understood by others, notably José and her brother-in-law Germán.

While the most significant links of this first novel with Quiroga's later works are to be found in the theme of solitude and the development of the solitary character, other major recurrent themes are suggested. In the character of Elisa's mother we find that desire for freedom dominating many later characters, including Tadea. A major theme of the Tadea novels, the repressive child-rearing attitudes of Spain in the 1920s, is mentioned briefly in *Sonorous Solitude,* as is the child's interest in reading. (Elisa from time to time quotes from the poets Gustavo Adolfo Bécquer, Rubén Darío and Pedro Salinas.) The house where Elisa is raised is undoubtedly the same one in Santander that Quiroga will describe more fully in the Tadea novels. The author's love of Galicia, more obvious in later works, is at least briefly mentioned when Elisa and Diego visit Galicia and Portugal on their honeymoon. Although the style of *Sonorous Solitude* is frequently exaggerated, there are foreshadowings of the abundant poetic descriptions in *Northwind* and *Blood*.

In discussing the Spanish novel of the late 1940s and early 1950s, several critics have made comparisons between Quiroga and Miguel Delibes. Hoyos points out that both young novelists wrote weak first novels.[6] De Nora similarly suggests that both won the Nadal Prize with inferior novels but later did very well.[7] A certain parallel in their development as novelists continues over the years in that both of them voluntarily remained somewhat isolated from the Spanish literary scene and wrote as they pleased, without attachment to any school.[8] Although their novelistic techniques and themes are generally quite different, a comparison between Quiroga's *Something's Happening in the Street* and Delibes' later *Cinco horas con Mario* (*Five Hours with Mario,* 1966) is frequently made.[9] To our knowledge, however, no one has as yet noticed the similar tie between Delibes' *El camino* (*The Path,* 1950) and *Sonorous Solitude.* In the later novel, Delibes suggests that each person has a path in life which he is intended to follow; the child character of the novel, Daniel, is disturbed because he believes that he is being forced to abandon the path that was intended for him. Quiroga also emphasizes the metaphor. Elisa's brother-in-law Germán, who is unrealistically sensitive to the young woman's inner feelings and needs, tells Teresa that she and Elisa have had different paths in life, Teresa's being wide and easy, but Elisa's being narrow and difficult: "She had to clear the path, although in doing it, her hands bled. Elisa believed that her path would always be narrow and difficult, filled with thorns" (*S,* 189). In this way Germán explains Elisa's inability at first to accept José and their happiness. Later, when their happiness is no longer possible, Elisa herself develops the same metaphor, asserting that the path she must follow in renouncing love is the straight path of duty. The symbolism of the path of life is, of course, not a new one, being based upon Christian teachings, but it is perhaps more than mere coincidence that Delibes should develop the theme in his novel which appeared so shortly after Quiroga's.

II Northwind

Although *Sonorous Solitude* did indicate Quiroga's potential as a novelist to some extent and attract limited critical attention, it was the prize-winning *Viento del norte (Northwind)* that brought national recognition to the young writer. Set in rural Galicia, *Northwind* relates the story of Marcela, a peasant girl, and Alvaro, a wealthy landowner. An illegitimate child, Marcela is abandoned as an infant by her mother, who had been prevented from killing the baby when she was born. Alvaro, a kindly, scholarly man, brings the child into his home to be raised by Ermitas, an elderly servant who had been Alvaro's own nursemaid. As Marcela grows up, she is befriended by Alvaro's young cousin, Lucía, who lives on a neighboring estate. When Lucía is in danger of contracting tuberculosis, from which her sister is dying, Marcela accompanies the older girl on a lengthy stay at a distant farm. When Marcela returns to La Sagreira, Alvaro, now in his fifties, discovers that the adolescent red-haired girl is very beautiful and also, from Lucía's influence, somewhat more refined than the average peasant woman.

At first Alvaro attempts to overcome the attraction he feels for Marcela, but finally decides that his love for her is not shameful. At the insistence of his aunt, he sends Marcela away to a convent school for two years and then marries her. A timid man in many ways, Alvaro makes no effort either to win Marcela's affection or to convince her that he loves her. Marcela in turn, has always been a silent, uncommunicative person, and accepts the marriage because she feels she has no choice and must do what the master wishes. When Marcela becomes pregnant, there is a momentary possibility that Alvaro will break through the barrier and establish a bond of affection with his wife, but he is unable to do so. The birth of their son does not, therefore, bring them together. Marcela, who loves the child deeply as the only part of her life that has ever been truly hers, feels that she has been treated merely as a vehicle for producing a son. Alvaro, on the other hand, is afraid that Marcela is not capable of raising the child in a manner suitable to his social class.

The conflict between husband and wife comes to a climax following the funeral of Alvaro's uncle, Don Enrique. Marcela appears in the village dressed in peasant clothes, and Alvaro feels that she has deliberately humiliated him. Once they are home, he starts to drink. The two fight, and Marcela calls him an old man. Hurt and angry he goes out on horseback, in spite of a storm. He is thrown from his horse and, as a result of the accident, is paralyzed and confined to a wheelchair.

Alvaro accepts his fate with relative serenity. For many years he had been working on a book of Galician history, and his physical handicap does not interfere with his writing. He finds satisfaction in the time spent with his little son, and he comes to treat Marcela with greater understanding than ever before. At his insistence, Marcela adopts the custom of spending each afternoon at Cora with Alvaro's aunt and cousin Lucía, leaving Alvaro to visit with his friends, the doctor, the priest, and the judge. The young judge, however, is attracted to Marcela and begins to visit Cora instead of La Sagreira in an effort to seduce her. At first Marcela neither realizes his attentions nor is aware that Alvaro is alone in the afternoon. When the judge informs her of the latter situation in front of Lucía and her mother, Marcela knows that she has lost their sympathy. But, in defiance, she decides to make one more afternoon trip to Cora; it is on that final occasion that the judge makes advances to her. Suddenly she realizes how much she loves and respects Alvaro and hurries home to him, only to find that he has died. The novel ends as Marcela enters the house and, identifying the odor of burning paper as being Alvaro's book that has fallen in the fireplace, knows that he is dead. With his death she has lost her sole defender and protector.

Northwind is unquestionably a much better novel than *Sonorous Solitude*. Quiroga develops the story more slowly and carefully with a particularly skillful handling of the passage of time. Although she continues dominantly to present her characters externally from the point of view of a narrator in the third person, she avoids the superficial stereotypes that abounded in the earlier novel. Marcela and Alvaro are particularly well-rounded, believable characters, as are many of the secondary figures. Also notably improved is her capacity for describing her setting and evoking an atmosphere. On the other hand, this second novel bears a number of strong resemblances to *Sonorous Solitude*. Here again Quiroga divides her novel into parts, each representing a phase in the protagonist's life. Part I takes us from Marcela's birth to her trip with Lucía; Part II ends as Alvaro decides to send Marcela to the boarding school; Part III recounts Marcela's reaction to school, her marriage, and the birth of her son; Part IV includes Alvaro's accident and his death.

Even more striking, however, are similarities in characters. Marcela, like Elisa, suffers rejection and loneliness as a child, is unable to communicate her innermost feelings, and is apparently condemned to a life of solitude in her early twenties. As with Elisa's reaction after learning of Diego's alleged death, Marcela finds that it is too late for her to express her feelings to the man who loved her. Like Elisa's mother, Marcela yearns for freedom, suffering particularly when she must wear a heavy school uniform and be shut in behind the convent walls. She is much happier running barefoot through the countryside. Also as in *Sonorous Solitude,* Quiroga introduces here a May-December marriage, although with a greater discrepancy in ages and without a deep sense of love and understanding that José and Elisa share.

The critical reaction to *Northwind* has been frequently negative, with many reviewers categorizing the work as anachronistic in style, plot, setting, and characterization. The most frequent judgment is that Quiroga picked up where Pardo Bazán had left off. Alborg holds that *Northwind* is better than Pardo Bazán's novels, but that regional works filled with local color are no longer of interest.[10] Corrales Egea agrees that it is rural naturalism but feels that *Northwind* lacks the social protest of the nineteenth-century novels.[11] De Nora also finds the work to be anachronistic, but describes it as medieval or romantic rather than naturalistic.[12] On the other hand, Entrambasaguas, who greeted each of Quiroga's novels with enthusiasm, has high praise for *Northwind,* finding it neither imitative of Pardo Bazán's works nor lacking in new techniques,[13] and Brent considers it Quiroga's best novel up to and including *The Mask.*[14] Not surprisingly, the reaction in Galicia was positive. Correa Calderón rejects the prevailing notion of the postwar period that all novels must deal with the city and further accepts Quiroga's Galicia as being from the present, not the past.[15] In fact, he feels that the novelist has created such a living fictional world that the reader almost believes that he will be attending Alvaro's funeral.

To be sure, *Northwind* is not a perfect novel, and in it Quiroga has not yet reached the mastery of innovative structural techniques of later works. In its linear structure and its traditional narrative form, the novel is not unlike certain nineteenth-century works.

Moreover, the final section of the novel, with Alvaro's accident and death, verges on the melodramatic. But critics who classified it as naturalism in the manner of Pardo Bazán or as romanticism were not correct. As Quiroga herself has pointed out, her characters are capable of change and are multifaceted. In Quiroga's rural Galicia, the characters are not trapped by the sociological situation in which they find themselves, as were Pardo Bazán's characters in her great rural novels, nor is there a general level of degeneracy and decadence. Marcela, in spite of her humble origins and the open hostility of other servants, is capable of raising her own cultural and social level. In a purely naturalistic work, she would surely have reverted to the immorality of her mother. In a romantic work, on the other hand, we might have had a Cinderella story in which she could have totally overcome her educational and social disadvantages. And, were the novel romantic as De Nora contends, Alvaro would not have had such a realistic blend of strong points and weak points to his character. It is hard to imagine Alvaro, the fifty-year-old bachelor with the weak eyesight and the total devotion to his scholarly work, as a romantic hero! It is likewise not necessarily true that *Northwind* is anachronistic in its plot and setting. Quiroga does not pinpoint the time setting for the novel, but La Sagreira has electricity, so it is unlikely that the author intended the action to take place in the past century. In all probability, Quiroga was attempting to give a realistic portrayal of prewar Galicia, where the master-servant relationship on the landed estates had not varied substantially over a period of centuries. In speaking of social class distinctions later described in *I Write Your Name,* Quiroga has commented that an almost feudal societal structure still existed in Spain into the 1920s and 1930s and was one of the causes of the Civil War.[16] Even today the traveler in rural Galicia has the sense of moving into the past as he or she sees the black-garbed peasants working in the fields with hand-drawn or ox-drawn plows.

As noted in Chapter 1, Quiroga herself feels a greater kinship to Valle-Inclán than to Pardo Bazán, and parallels exist between *Northwind* and the Galician works of the former writer. Like Valle-Inclán, Quiroga evokes legendary aspects of Galicia, recounting superstitions of the peasants. Similarly she emphasizes the poetic beauty of the landscape — the trees, the mountains, and the shore of the *rías* where the rivers meet the sea — and of the Galician weather — the frequent rain, the storms, the wind or *tumbalou-*

reiro. Some of her secondary characters bear a resemblance to certain types that Valle-Inclán described in the early twentieth century, notably Don Enrique. Alvaro's uncle, like Valle-Inclán's Don Juan Manuel Montenegro, is a patriarchal figure, proud of his virility, given to hunting, drinking, and illicit love affairs — but always conscious of the family honor and the virtue of his long-suffering wife. In Quiroga's work, however, there is no hint of Valle-Inclán's *esperpento,* no tendency to deliberately deform and satirize one's own characters. Quiroga appears to have drawn Don Enrique from reality and then treated him on a realistic level rather than taking him from the pages of Valle-Inclán's works.[17] The same observation might be made of the other characters, particularly those of the lower class, who are reminiscent of Valle-Inclán's Galicia, such as the vagabond Yago, Marcela's mother Matuxa, and Ermitas.

The principal strength of Quiroga in *Northwind,* as Lucile Delano has noted, is her character portrayal: "With a real talent for psychological analysis, for the creation of effective sensory images, and for the use of graphic figures of speech, she is able to produce personages that leave the reader with a very vivid impression."[18] This is indeed true of her two major figures, both of whom she develops slowly and carefully. Although Marcela tends to rise to an almost mythic level—Hoyos has called her a literary figure of impressive size[19] — in general both she and Alvaro are realistically-drawn characters. De Nora, whose response to *Northwind* is quite negative, states that Alvaro is a stereotype because of the conventionalism of his feelings, his reactions and mòtives.[20] But de Nora's judgment is not totally accurate; Alvaro stands out as an individual whose motivations are quite believable. If Quiroga is to be criticized for the portrayal of Alvaro, it is for her presentation of his character, particularly in the early chapters of the novel, more through an omniscient narrator than through his own actions or thoughts. In her later, more mature works, Quiroga often presents us with an inexplicable act on the part of a character and then probes retrospectively to uncover what led the character to do what he or she did. This type of in-depth analysis is lacking here because of the narrative structure, but the preparation for Alvaro's act — his marrying a girl more than thirty years his junior and not of his social class — is quite complete. Like Marcela, but to a lesser degree, Alvaro has trouble communicating with others, and, typical of many of Quiroga's characters, this problem may be the result of an isolated childhood, for his mother, too, died when he was very little. In his solitude, and reinforced by his years of study at the university in Santiago, he takes refuge in books and in writing; but this avocation merely deepens his isolation, for no one in his rural area understands his scholarly interests. Only when he visits his cousin Tula during her illness does he find someone with whom he can really talk. His uncle Enrique finds it very unmasculine to read books and chides Alvaro constantly in this respect. But Alvaro generally has greater difficulty being accepted by women than by men; in fact, they find him boring and make fun of him.[21]

Alvaro, then, is a solitary individual, like so many of Quiroga's characters. And, as she frequently points out, solitude is fine when one is at peace with oneself, but a serious psychological problem when one is not. In his thirties and forties Alvaro seems quite contented; his book, his hunting trips, the administration of his farm fill his days and give his life meaning. But as he enters his fifties, he begins to feel old and alone. At one point he invites his cousin Jorge to stay with him for several days to help fill the void. It is at this stage in his life that he notices Marcela and finds that he cannot get her out of his mind. His sudden discovery of her youthful beauty is made more believable by her absence from La Sagreira precisely during the years that she matured into womanhood. Alvaro is initially afraid that Marcela will ridicule him when she learns of his love, but it does not occur to him that he is being unfair to her in marrying her.

Marcela is a taciturn, and in some respects, untamed person. The explanation of her character is given in great detail through the course of the novel. Like Elisa or Tadea, she is made to feel unwelcome in the home where she lives as a child. She overhears servants suggest that she be sent to an orphanage and that the master only keeps her from a sense of charity. Even Ermitas, who loves her deeply, contributes to Marcela's bitterness by repeatedly telling her that she owes Alvaro everything: the bread she eats, the clothes she wears, the roof over her head. Marcela becomes increasingly resentful, because she feels that she works hard to earn her keep. The time she spends with Lucía raises her educational and cultural level, but this only tends to separate her more from the other servants and peasants. She does not belong in the class of the landowners, but she no longer fits in with the lower class even if they were to accept her. After her marriage to Alvaro, she feels that she is still his servant — that she has merely changed her name from maid to wife but that her subservient relationship to him remains the same. After his accident, she is overcome by a guilt which she cannot express, just as he cannot express to her his belief that he, and only he, was responsible. Only with Lucía is Marcela able to articulate some of her feelings; the loss of Lucía's sympathy at the end of the novel is, therefore, a serious blow.

Quiroga carefully and deliberately shows us the anguish of Alvaro and Marcela, evenhandedly giving us both sides of the story. The blame for the failure of the marriage is certainly a shared one. She skillfully juxtaposes their feelings so that we may understand the barrier that separates them. In this manner she prepares us for the explosion of hostility that finally finds expression in the fight precipitating Alvaro's accident. The landowner has two weak points: he puts a high value on his sense of dignity and he wants to forget his age. Marcela, in turn, has built up a bitter resentment because of the gratitude she is supposed to feel toward Alvaro. She outrages Alvaro's sense of dignity by going in peasant dress to the funeral. He, in revenge, tramples on her greatest sensitivity when he tells her that she does not appreciate all the things he has done for her. In the heat of argument, she then calls him an old man. This final insult is more than he can bear and, in anger, he responds irrationally by going horseback riding in a storm. In terms of plot development, the riding accident is rather forced, but with respect to the psychological development of her characters, the accident becomes plausible.

In *Northwind*, to a greater degree than any of her other works, Quiroga emphasizes the natural setting, giving detailed descriptions of the Galician landscape.[22] Frequently aspects of nature are personified, with parallel relationships established between them and the human characters. For Alvaro, Marcela is like the golden and reddish soil, Tula is like a cypress tree, and his cousin Dorila has the arrogance and beauty of the mountain (*N*, 129). A description of the fierce northwind, the *tumbaloureiro* (*N*, 223), precedes the "human storm" (*N*, 227), the fight between Alvaro and Marcela. For Marcela, Alvaro comes to be symbolized by a laurel tree in whose shade she finds protection. The novel ends with a statement that the laurel has been downed. The poetic treatment of nature continues in *Blood*, where the narrator of the novel is a chestnut tree. This narrative device is also linked to a scene in *Northwind* when Alvaro, following the birth of his son, finds himself with an awakened interest in his ancestry. Suddenly the chairs and the bed, which have witnessed the joys and sorrows of his family through many generations, seem to whisper to him these stories from the past (*N*, 197–99).

III   Blood

Clearly Quiroga's choice of a tree as narrator in *La sangre (Blood)* is the one aspect of the novel that first attracts the reader's attention and which has most stimulated critical commentaries. For some critics the decision to relate the lives of four generations of a family from the perspective of the chestnut tree outside the ancestral home was a true poetic inspiration. Alborg, for example, who had viewed *Northwind* quite negatively, found *Blood* to be free both of regionalism and of old realism.[23] On the other hand, de Nora, while stating that most writers had praised the novel, finds *Blood* to be romantic and weak.[24] Most of the critics who found fault with the novel suggested, like de Nora, that *Blood* was romantic, but at least one critic attacked the work quite violently for being naturalistic.[25]

Although at first glance these two viewpoints — that the novel was romantic and that it was naturalistic — appear antithetical, on closer analysis one finds some truth in both assertions. If one wishes to label the personification of nature as a romantic characteristic, then clearly *Blood* has "romantic" elements. The chestnut tree itself is a person, capable of relating the story to us in the first person. From the tree's perspective, the human characters have close ties to animals and plants — and vice versa. There is, in this poetic, lyrical treatment of nature, a certain link with romanticism. But the story related to us by the tree is anything but romantic. Montoliu, in labeling the work naturalistic, calls it the "chronicle of hereditary abnormalities of the children born to four couples."[26] This is a somewhat exaggerated view, but certainly the novel does show, as Hoyos states, the "inheritance of a blood that unites and enslaves."[27] Quiroga's choice of title would indicate her intention to develop such a theme, and the gradual degeneracy and destruction of a family that she shows in the novel could well be considered a naturalistic theme.

In this respect it is interesting to read the prologue that Quiroga

wrote in 1952, the same year *Blood* was published, to preface her
husband's study of the lineage of Pardo Bazán.[28] She speaks there
strongly of inheritance and suggests that no one is born without a
"prepersonality." She supports the concept of genealogical studies,
the kind of historical work in which Dalmiro de la Válgoma
specializes, suggesting that individuals "in spite of themselves,
respond to the blood that gives them life and to the environment
and even the landscape that surrounds them." It must be noted that
this opinion is quite in opposition to Quiroga's frequently expressed views on the autonomy of literary characters, let alone
human beings. In *Blood* she seems to have developed her characters
at least partially in conformity to this deterministic theory of
inheritance in a manner not typical of her novelistic production as a
whole. Her commitment to the inheritance concept is not so complete as it might be, however. The chestnut tree, because of its lack
of mobility and its limited range of vision, has a limited knowledge
of the humans it watches, but ironically, the humans, too, have limited perspectives. The members of the family themselves erroneously believe that they are marked by a certain destiny. Xavier,
for example, feels that he killed his cousin Donato in part because
of a violent streak inherited from his grandfather Amador, who
had killed his wife.[29] But the tree and the readers know that the
story Xavier heard is not true.

Most critics, in speaking of literary influences on Quiroga's
works, mention Faulkner, but only in the novels following *Blood*.
Curiously they have not noted that this particular novel, with its
blend of lyricism and naturalism, its constant shifting from past to
present, and its treatment of a decaying aristocracy is very closely
linked to the North American novelist. *Blood* does, in fact, have
certain marked parallels with *Absalom, Absalom!,* a novel with
which Quiroga is personally familiar.[30] Like *Blood,* Faulkner's
novel traces several generations of a family, culminating in the end
of the family line. In each generation he shows us the master-
servant relationships and the love-hate conflicts. The hereditary
traits in Faulkner's characters that link parent to child are even
more pronounced than in Quiroga's work, but both novelists
emphasize the possibility of identifying illegitimate children by
such family traits. The crimes in both novels are also related.
Quiroga's Xavier kills his cousin Donato, who is a homosexual, to
prevent his sister from marrying him. In *Absalom, Absalom!*

Henry Sutphen kills his illegitimate half-brother Charles to prevent him from marrying their sister Judith. In both cases the assassins never recover from their crimes, being forced initially into hiding and broken in spirit ever after. These parallels are not to suggest that Quiroga intentionally imitated Faulkner in *Blood,* but rather that her third novel was not so "nineteenth century" as some Spanish critics claimed.

Quiroga feels that the negative reaction to *Blood* at the time of its publication may be attributed to the dominant realism of the period. Critics were simply unprepared for a poetic novel. She notes with a certain pride that fifteen years later, when Gabriel García Márquez published his bestselling *Cien años de soledad (One Hundred Years of Solitude),* critics in France suggested that the Colombian novelist had been influenced by Quiroga's *Blood.*[31] In fact, although the later novel develops a level of fantasy, myth, and magic realism that sets it quite apart from the more realistic *Blood,* there are certain notable relationships between the two works. Some of these may be attributed to their common ties to Faulkner, perhaps specifically to *Absalom, Absalom!* For example, the narration of events during several generations of a family, ending with the extinction of the clan, and the fluctuation between past and present in that narration are Faulknerian techniques adopted by both Quiroga and García Márquez. Perhaps more directly related to *Blood,* however, is the use of the chestnut tree in *One Hundred Years of Solitude.* After José Arcadio Buendía goes mad, he is tied to the chestnut tree; following his death, his ghost, visible only to his wife, remains under the tree. The tree thus almost becomes a character from the perspective of those who see not the ghost but Ursula talking to the chestnut. In a sense, the ghostly chestnut witnesses the passage of time and the growing decadence of the family much as does Quiroga's tree. Another possible link between Quiroga and García Márquez is found in the latter's treatment of Meme. When the girl's lover is killed, she responds to the tragedy by never speaking again and by becoming virtually immobile. In *Blood,* Quiroga's idiot character Eladio does the same when Amalia is dying, but even more parallel is the situation of Liberata in *The Sick Woman* who becomes both motionless and mute after learning that her fiancé has married another woman. The similarity between Quiroga and García Márquez in these aspects may be mere coincidence, but it is an area worthy of further study.

Blood does not contain a genealogy of characters as editions of Faulkner's novels sometimes do. While such an analysis is not as essential for Quiroga's novel as for Faulkner's works, it would nevertheless be helpful. *Blood* does not pretend to be a historical novel and therefore does not give us any kind of accurate chronology for the events that happen to the family. The only two dates mentioned are 1900, the year of Pastor's birth, and 1933, the year of death of both Lorenzo and the chestnut tree. The following, then, is a genealogy proposed by the present writer. First there is Amador, a seaman, who marries María Fernanda, a young woman from Oviedo, sometime in the 1850s. She gives birth to Amalia while he is off to sea and later dies as a result of a second pregnancy. He leaves the little girl in the care of the servants and does not return home until his grandson is born. By burning the family papers, he establishes himself as the beginning of the family line.

Amalia grows up as an orphan and, like her father, is prone to fits of violence. She is married to Efrén when she is only fifteen. Efrén is a relatively weak man; as the second son in his family, he feels that the older brother has been the favorite. He agrees to have his children use Amalia's family name rather than his own. During the 1870s they have three children: Gertrudis, Xavier, and Jacoba. Gertrudis is raised in part by Efrén's sister in the city; she marries and stays there. Efrén dies before Xavier and Jacoba are established in life.

Xavier initially appears to be a true descendant of Amador and Amalia, having inherited their strong character. As a teenager, he fathers an illegitimate child, Vicente. Vicente's mother Justina, a servant, dies in childbirth, and he is raised by Justina's husband. Xavier loses his forcefulness after killing his effeminate cousin Donato to prevent his marriage to Jacoba, who enters a convent. Xavier marries Dolores, Donato's sister, a cold and calculating woman who makes Amalia's last days miserable and later tries to poison Xavier. Their son Pastor is born at the turn of the century. Dolores dies when Vicente forces her to drink the "medicine" she has prepared for Xavier.

Pastor spends much of his childhood away from his parents, either with his aunt Gertrudis or in boarding school. He does not feel the attachment to the family home that his ancestors did and begins to sell parcels of the property. He marries an actress, Angeles, and their son, Lorenzo, is born in 1925. Pastor espouses liberal causes, claiming to believe in equality, but he treats the servants harshly. He is unfaithful to Angeles and turns her from a happy person to a melancholy one. His relationship with his half-brother Vicente is an ambivalent one.

Lorenzo, a precocious, sensitive child who loves nature is the last of the family line. When the chestnut tree is felled at the end of the novel, he is crushed to death.

In the course of the novel, Quiroga analyzes in some depth the individual dramas of each generation of family members, along with those of the servants. While she never breaks with her basic narrative device, faithfully presenting only what the tree could have witnessed, she does give some flexibility to this perspective by allowing the tree to overhear conversations among the human characters. At the heart of each of these dramas is love and passion, often coupled with the same lack of communication that the author previously emphasized in *Sonorous Solitude* and *Northwind*. As the tree observes, "Thus they go on, deceiving themselves and deceiving others, running through their lives without stopping a moment to unearth the truth about other people" (*B,* 125). In *Northwind,* Quiroga develops only one scene in which husband and wife finally unleash their hostilities and frustrations. In *Blood,* there are several such scenes, notably the series of quarrels between Amalia and Efrén. In some respects the conflict between these two is similar to that between Alvaro and Marcela in *Northwind.* He is the refined young man from the city; she, the uncivilized country girl. He accuses her of being "common," and she accuses him of not being a man. Ultimately, however, they find that they love and need one another; when he is dying, she is willing to defy God to save him. The violence of their relationship is obviously healthier than the cold hatred of Dolores that would permit her to slowly poison her husband. But in all of these cases, Quiroga does give some psychological explanation for the action of her characters in addition to the hereditary one. Amalia is responding in part to her being abandoned by her father after her mother's death. Efrén is imprisoned by his feelings of hatred and envy stemming from his disadvantaged position as second son. Dolores' innate cruelty turns to hatred when she fears that Xavier will disinherit her son, Pastor, in favor of the illegitimate son, Vicente.

Quiroga's insistence on hereditary traits in *Blood* deflects, however, from her usual careful psychological development of character. Jacoba, for example, has the same step and the same saintly character as her grandmother María Fernanda. Amalia, Xavier, Vicente, Pastor, and Lorenzo all bear some resemblance to Amador. Xavier inherits his initial strong will from his mother and his later weakness from his father. Pastor has the good traits that come from Xavier-Amalia-Amador, but unfortunately blended with Dolores' cruelty. At several points in the novel the tree observes that the generations are inexorably bound together and that one does not die entirely, for one lives on in the children and grandchildren. In that the tree frequently defines human characteristics in terms of plants and animals, it typically notes that the people in the house can only produce other people like themselves, just as only chestnut trees can grow from chestnuts (*B*, 20).

The resemblance of one generation to another is one of the devices Quiroga uses to justify the fluidity of time throughout the novel. The tree is constantly reminded of Amador while talking of Vicente or prompted to jump ahead to the arrival of Angeles while recounting the life of Amalia. In a Proustian fashion, the narrative may flow from present to past because a particular sight or smell has evoked a bygone moment. More often, however, the tree will simply refer ahead to events completely out of chronology. A reference to the "terrible night" (*B*, 154) when Dolores dies comes many pages ahead of the event itself (*B*, 269). This technique is particularly noticeable with respect to Lorenzo, to whom the tree refers frequently starting with the fourth page of the novel. The reason for this is twofold. Lorenzo is the human being the tree most loves, so the tree's affection leads it to think about the child with the chestnut eyes. Additionally, Quiroga wants to emphasize the little boy's sensitive and loving personality so that we will feel his death more at the end of the novel. The end, which in itself is as abrupt as the final lines of *Northwind*,[32] has actually been anticipated very early in the novel when the tree juxtaposes a story of how the people cut down an oak in the past with a description of Lorenzo playing in its own branches in the present (*B*, 42–43). The tree, of course, does not anticipate its own death during the narration, although the themes of life, death, and time are dominant ones throughout the novel. When the final blow has been struck on the chestnut's trunk and the tree begins to fall, its consciousness ends as does the narrative itself. At that point people are shouting at the child to get out of the way of the falling tree.

Quiroga's intention at the conclusion of the novel is to show the end of a family and the end of a culture. Although some critics felt that *Blood* was not historical and should have been,[33] the author does give some indication of societal changes brought by the twentieth century and an indication of the class conflict that would reach its climax in the impending Civil War. She gives fuller expression to this theme in *I Write Your Name.*

Blood is related to Quiroga's other·works primarily in the type of characters it introduces — orphans and solitary figures, such as Vicente and later Angeles — but set apart from the majority of her novels both for its tendency toward naturalism and the intense lyricism of its fusion of nature and humanity. The narrator equates people to trees. Efrén's father is a willow; Amalia, a pine (*B*, 60–61). Dying people are like fallen tree trunks (*B*, 177, 279). People are also like animals: Efrén and Amalia fight like a cock and a hen (*B*, 50); Amador is like a fox (*B*, 22); and men, in general, are wolves (*B*, 114). To reinforce these relationships, Quiroga personifies elements of nature. The dog Toula is almost like another human character. The chestnut itself is capable of love and, in fact, it is the tree's love of the house that causes it to grow in that direction, ultimately leading to its death when its roots threaten the structure. When the death sentence for the chestnut has been pronounced, all nature voices its sorrow (*B*, 340).

Blood is a much more innovative work than either *Sonorous Solitude* or *Northwind* and further removed from the traditional linear narrative. In this sense it stands as a work of transition between the two early novels and experimental works to follow.

CHAPTER 3

The Short Novels

E LENA Quiroga has dedicated herself almost exclusively to writing full-length novels. The one notable exception to this is her volume of novelettes *Plácida, la joven y otras narraciones (The Young Plácida and Other Stories)*. The collection, published in 1956, includes three short novels, two of which originally appeared in 1953 in the series of popular, short novels "La Novela del Sábado." These two, *Trayecto uno (Bus One)* and *La otra ciudad (The Other City)*, are quite different in technique from the early novels analyzed in the preceding chapter and might in turn be considered transitional works between *Blood* and the experimental novels that followed. The title novelette of the collection, however, dates from somewhat later, falling chronologically after *La careta (The Mask)*.

I Bus One

The first novelette, *Bus One* takes place in Madrid in the afternoon of January 15, 1953. The date is indicated to us by the jottings of Anuncia, a university student who boards a bus at Moncloa and traverses the city. The entire action of the novelette is that one-way bus trip, with the reader being given a glimpse into the lives and problems of various passengers who get on and off the bus, and of the driver and conductor. The bus line is Cartagena-Princesa-Moncloa (via Ferraz), a route that would pass by the house where Quiroga lived at the time she wrote the story; she does, in fact, dedicate *Bus One,* to her fellow passengers on that line.

In *Bus One* Quiroga is quite successful in creating the atmosphere of the bus and of making the reader experience the ride across the city. She emphasizes the motion of the bus, the starts and stops. She carefully choreographs the boarding and departure of the various passengers to give an illusion of reality. School children, for example, ride only a short distance, as might be expected. A young dandy, obviously a foreigner, gets on at Moncloa, the university stop, and off on the Gran Vía, where he might logically go seeking excitement. A florist's delivery boy gets on in the business district and off in a fashionable section of the city. She heightens the realism of the trip itself by occasional references to the landmarks the bus passes — the Plaza de España, Cibeles, the entrance to the Retiro — and to the shop windows and signs one would see from the bus. She evokes the city and the bus ride so effectively that readers who know Madrid well can imagine that they, too, are passengers.

Quiroga's primary intention in *Bus One,* however, is not so much to create the atmosphere of the city as to depict the passengers who board the bus. In writing of *Blood,* one critic suggested that her technique there was behaviorist or an objective representation of what might have been viewed by a camera.[1] The subjective, lyric element in *Blood* largely refutes this assessment, which might more correctly be made of *Bus One.* The novelette is, in fact, the work of Quiroga's which bears the greatest relationship to social realism and, in its technique, it might well be compared to Cela's *La colmena (The Hive)* and Luis Romero's *La noria (The Treadmill).* Cela's novel, published in 1951, and Romero's, which won the Nadal Prize that same year, have been labeled the first multiple protagonist novels of postwar Spain.[2] Choosing Madrid as his setting, Cela uses a fragmentary structure to show the lives of a cross section of society. Romero has a similar intent, but sets the action in Barcelona and develops a more organized structure; in each, the central figure has some contact with a secondary character who in turn becomes the central figure of the following section. Like these two novels, Quiroga's *Bus One* introduces a number of characters of comparable importance rather than a single protagonist. Her choice of the shorter novelette form allows her to develop the multiple protagonist approach within the realistic and unifying framework of the bus ride, without resorting to either the artificial chain structure developed by Romero or the more complex mosaic structure of Cela. Quiroga's approach, in this sense, is not unlike the concept expressed by John Dos Passos in his title *Manhattan Transfer,* implying that the lives of many individuals intersect on the bus lines of the city, or that of the Brazilian multiple-protagonist novel *Caminhos cruzados (Crossed Paths)* by Erico Veríssimo. Within the context of an hour's bus ride across the city, fourteen characters or groups of characters briefly come in contact with one another; as their paths cross, the readers and, to some extent, the fellow passengers glimpse their individual dramas.

While *Bus One* is obviously related in technique to *The Hive* and *The Treadmill,* both of which have been categorized as social novels by Pablo Gil Casado in *La novela social española (1942-1968),* it is doubtful that Quiroga's novelette would fulfill all six requirements that he outlines for the genre. Quiroga's work does have a collective hero and presents an objective picture of various levels of society, including some reference to suffering and economic problems, but the element of strong social criticism or denunciation which Gil Casado finds present in the novels of social realism is lacking here.[3] The little boy on the bus with his nursemaid is obviously sick and may die, but his father's employer willingly gives salary advances so that the parents may buy the child his needed medicine. The laborer regrets his lot in life and dreams of winning the lottery, but there is no indication that he is being exploited by anyone. Fermín's wife knows that her husband has been taken away by the police, and she is on the bus to go to the jail to seek his freedom, but we know that Fermín committed a crime. The problems of these characters may be related to general social and economic ills, but there is no effort on the part of the author to suggest that they are victims of social injustice. The lack of denunciation is further reinforced by the attitude of Anuncia, one of the two characters who most serve to give unity to the story. Anuncia has experienced something of an existential awakening as a result of poetry she has been reading — specifically that of Pedro Salinas. Suddenly she is so conscious of her own existence and that of others that she leaves the university in the middle of a lecture and boards the bus. Experiencing life on a new level, she looks at the people around her with new eyes and attempts to understand them and their feelings. Her sense of empathy with her fellow human beings is quite different from the alienation and social criticism that one finds in Martín Marco of *The Hive,* for example.

Quiroga develops the many characters in *Bus One* through a skillful use of dialogue, first-person interior monologues, and third-person narrative, generally from the perspective of one of the characters. She captures realistically the speech of the various characters or groups of characters, being particularly successful with the chatter of the school girls and the communication problems of a deaf passenger. Within the thoughts of the passengers, we are given glimpses of their lives. The nursemaid, for example, recalls conversations between the anguished father and mother about the health of the little boy. Anuncia, perceiving the scent of violets that the florist's delivery boy is carrying, is transported by the smell to her own past and, in a flashback, recalls her life with her grandparents. The third-person passages sometimes merely recount objectively what is happening and sometimes give us, in an indirect style, the reaction of one character to another. Anuncia, in particular, observes and thinks about other passengers, as does Blas, the conductor. But we are also given the perspective of other passengers. For example, Margot, a well-dressed, attractive woman, gives us her opinion of the man seated next to her. The laborer, in turn, gives us his impression of Margot. The characters least likely to observe other passengers are those most immersed in their own problems — the nursemaid, who can only think of the sick child, and Fermín's wife, who cannot get her mind off her husband's being in jail.

Among the narrative devices used by Quiroga in the novelette are two also found in *The Hive*. Like Cela, Quiroga sometimes gives two or more perspectives on the same episode. For example, we have several commentaries on Margot's boarding the bus — almost knocking over the deaf man in her haste. Also, Quiroga, like Cela, gives unity to the narrative through a contrapuntal technique, as when two or more characters will notice and then think about the same shop window or the same scene viewed from the bus.

Among the characters and situations developed by Quiroga in *Bus One* are at least two repeated in later works. One of the school children loves to read but must do so in hiding; at one time her cousins were not allowed to play with her because of the books she had read Her father, not wanting to discourage her entirely but shocked by the love stories she has had access to, insists that she read *Platery y yo (Platero and I)* with him. The child finds Juan Ramón Jiménez' book to be exceedingly dull. Anuncia's memories indicate that she is an orphan, raised by relatives; unlike most of Quiroga's orphaned characters, however, Anuncia feels that her grandparents loved her, even though she was sometimes ashamed of them. In *Bus One,* for the first time Quiroga creates the atmos-

phere of the city and concentrates on urban social classes. The
short novel is interesting in its structure and quite successful in
evoking realistically both the background of Madrid and the cast of
characters.

II   The Other City

Also set in Madrid, *La otra ciudad (The Other City),* like *Bus
One,* contains some realistic descriptions of the urban center and
the activities there, but the number of characters is greatly reduced
and the focus more on the subjective reality of individual characters than on the external, objective reality associated with the social
novel. The "other city" of the title is a cemetery just outside
Madrid, and the four characters are Tomás, the cemetery keeper;
his two sons, Esteban and Marcos; and Esteban's fiancée, Cruz. In
a structure very similar to that developed in *Something's Happening in the Street,* Quiroga constantly shifts among the perspectives
of these four characters. Most passages are written in the indirect
third person that Faulkner frequently used to reveal the inner
thoughts of his characters, but the novelette also includes passages
in the first person, sometimes in a stream-of-consciousness style.
This is particularly true of Marcos, the best developed of the four
characters and the one most inclined to evoke the past. In one
passage significantly revealing his character, Marcos imagines himself being interviewed by a psychiatrist and carries on a dialogue
with himself in the first and second persons.

The Other City is divided into two parts, each containing three
chapters. In the first part each chapter is written from the perspective of a different character: Tomás, Esteban, and Marcos, in that
order. Esteban is the son who never feared the cemetery and who
remains with his father. Marcos, on the other hand, was always
uncomfortable in the graveyard. An intelligent child, he was urged
to continue his education by the local priest, who helped finance his
studies. Marcos is now a doctor and only occasionally drives out to
visit his father. In the first two chapters of the second part, the
perspective shifts among these three characters and Cruz, a telephone operator. The final chapter is devoted entirely to Marcos.

The realistic backdrop of life in Madrid is particularly evident in
the sections relating to Esteban and Cruz. Quiroga gives us a detailed description of the telephone switchboard and Cruz's work,

with the telephone operators leaving their job in the afternoon while their boyfriends wait outside the building for them. Esteban and Cruz go to the movies, taking the subway and bus. In a minimum of space the author creates the atmosphere of the early evening in Madrid with its bustling activity. Her greatest achievement along these lines is the second chapter of the first part, where Esteban attends the *verbena* or popular festival on the eve of San Cayetano in the proletarian Lavapiés section of the city. This particular scene has been highly praised by both Fernández Almagro and Entrambasaguas.[4] The latter has termed *The Other City* a "true masterpiece" and feels that in the Lavapiés description Quiroga has uncovered "the soul of Madrid, as if she were led by the hand of Galdós." In her ability to evoke both the confusion of the celebration and the hostilities that arise among the people there, Quiroga foreshadows a similar scene in Luis Martín Santos' *Tiempo de silencio (Time of Silence).*

Of the four characters, Cruz is the one most closely related to characters in Quiroga's other works. Later in *The Sick Woman* and *The Young Plácida,* Quiroga again develops the role of the telephone operator; more significantly, however, Cruz is once again an orphaned child who cannot communicate her innermost feelings to other people. When Esteban takes her to meet his brother Marcos, a scene presented via a flashback, he is astonished to learn details of Cruz's life that she had never been able to mention to him. Cruz responds to Marcos the way that Elisa in *Sonorous Solitude* had reacted to José, suddenly discovering a person to whom she can unburden her thoughts and concerns. Esteban questions the reason for this reaction, and Cruz explains that a doctor is like a priest — someone to whom one may confess one's life and thoughts.

Esteban and Tomás are not as well developed as Cruz and Marcos, although Entrambasaguas has found Esteban to be typically Madrilenian.[5] The young man plans to marry Cruz, although he finds from time to time that he is distracted by other women, the kind that he meets at the dances and festivals that Cruz is not interested in attending. Tomás is in large part characterized by his job and his tendency to immerse himself in the graveyard and the tombstones to such an extent that the people buried there are more real to him than the living down below in the city. Despite his isolation and lack of education, he is a wise man, and it is his wisdom that Marcos, the educated son, finds himself seeking in his own hour of self-doubt.

Marcos has become a well-known pediatrician. When his mother died, he was in France delivering a paper at a scholarly meeting, a fact which continues to disturb him. He is even more disturbed by his failures as a doctor — the children he has been unable to save. Within the passages of his thoughts there are interspersed the comments of parents who feel that Marcos abandoned them when their child was beyond hope; the reader, of course, knows that Marcos felt these tragedies so deeply that he could not bear to see the dying child or the parents' grief.

In writing of *Blood,* at least one critic suggested that Quiroga was the long-awaited Catholic novelist of Spain.[6] In her novel he found that human anguish that priests confront and, along with the human suffering, a constant presence of the cross and religious values hovering in the background. In *The Other City* the Catholic theme moves to the foreground, for Marcos experiences a kind of conversion. Confronted daily by human suffering, he begins to doubt both his abilities as a doctor and his faith in God, but he seeks answers in the scriptures and in contact with the church. At one point he goes to confession to admit his doubts. When his father explains to him the earthly love of Esteban — his fidelity to Cruz in spite of his momentary attraction to other women — Marcos equates this with his own faith — his loyalty to the cross in spite of his moments of doubt. At the end of the novel, as Marcos drives back to the city via the Puente de Toledo, his face breaks into the same unconscious, radiant smile that we see on Tomás' face at the beginning of the work. This circular aspect in the structure of the novelette reinforces the idea expressed on several occasions that Marcos is much like his father and therefore presumably capable of finding the spiritual peace that Tomás feels. In his final thoughts Marcos equates God's love with that of Tomás, and certainly the religious symbolism of Cruz' name is apparent. Quite obviously Quiroga has intended a strong religious theme.

As in *Blood,* in *The Other City* Quiroga explores the mysteries of life and death.[7] The chestnut tree wonders at the symbolism of the cross and its meaning for mankind. Marcos suddenly discovers that he has grown up in the cemetery without seriously considering the message in what he saw about him. Now he stops to contemplate the cross and the inscription: *In hoc signo vincis* (By this sign, you will conquer).[8] He knows that his mother has finished her journey, but he does not know where death has taken her (*P,* 172). He has learned that life is short, that one does not have time to do everything (*P,* 168). The real truth in life is death — the death of a child (*P,* 201), but the cross is the sign that can conquer death (*P,* 197). Marcos realizes that his own life has been filled with fear, anguish, and emptiness (*P,* 196), in particular his fear of the graveyard. But through his awakened religious awareness, he finds release from fear and experiences a new peace.

Other comments about life within the novelette relate to a philosophy expressed in other works by Quiroga. As in *Sonorous Solitude,* the author evokes here the image of life as a path, this time expressed by Tomás: "Each of us must follow his own path" (*P,* 172). When Marcos hears the story of Cruz's life, he is moved to generalize: "That was a woman's life. A closed circuit: orphanhood, anguish, relative tranquillity of hard work; relative tranquillity, anguish, death" (*P,* 190). His words could serve as a synopsis for many dramas that Quiroga relates throughout her novels.

III The Young Plácida

Marcos' foregoing description of a woman's life applies to Plácida, central figure of the third short novel, except that Plácida dies in childbirth at the age of twenty, thus shortening the closed circuit of her existence. De Nora considers this title work the best of Quiroga's novelettes, seeing in it some of the most finely developed and psychologically penetrating pages of the author.[9] He finds also that *Plácida, la joven (The Young Plácida)* reiterates the theme of *The Sick Woman.* These are Quiroga's two works in which the main character has been drawn directly from life, and each is told, at least in part, from the perspective of a narrator who superficially appears to be the author herself. In both cases the narrator is a woman from the city, visiting a Galician village, who views the drama of another woman as a sympathetic outsider. Close examination, however, reveals that the narrator is not intended to be Quiroga and that the works are not autobiographical.

The Young Plácida begins, as does *Something's Happening in the Street,* with the announcement that the central character has died. The narrator, who is staying in rural Galicia with her older sister, Eduarda, writes to her husband both the news of Plácida's death and her own reaction to it. Admittedly the narration does not follow the usual epistolar form, however, as observed by the narrator herself when she comments, "Is this a letter or a way of suffering and putting the pain in order?" (*P,* 59). Although Plácida's little hut was adjacent to Eduarda's garden wall, the sisters do not learn of the young peasant woman's death until the following day. The narrator had never spoken to Plácida and now tries to recall when and where she might have seen her as she attempts to recount Plácida's life and death, some of it based on what people tell her and some based on her own conjectures. The narrator's sorrow is increased by her sense of guilt at having not noticed Plácida, not having offered her friendship or help. Interspersed with the story of Plácida, which does not follow chronological order, are digressions about the narrator's own background, the Galician countryside, and the reaction of the town to the death. As is typical of her works situated in Galicia, Quiroga develops many sensory images, stressing the sights and smells of the land and the sea.

Quiroga dedicates the novelette to Plácida and, through her, to all Galician peasant women. The author makes it clear that, except for her premature death, Plácida might be symbolic of all these poor but stoic women, forced to spend their lives at hard manual labor. The narrator suggests that she might have told Plácida how unfortunate she was, but that Plácida would not have understood: "To be poor or not to be lucky were for her matters like sex or her height or the dark color of her large, frightened eyes" (*P,* 22). Any other peasant woman, like one whom she observes during the annual vintage, might also serve as the subject of a novel. As the narrator writes to her husband: "Focus your spotlight on one of these lives, just a moment, stop it for yourself, and in the still beam it grows, becomes gigantic, you capture the shadows, you know, you understand that all the passions, the sadness, the misery of the world are in that insignificant common woman who wipes her nose on her hand. And in her the root of human tragedy. This is why she laughs" (*P,* 61).

Quiroga learned the story of the real Plácida at her husband's home in Nigrán. That this is the locale of the story is clear from the description in *The Young Plácida* of the lights in the nearby town of Bayona. The narrator in the novelette, however, is at the home of a half-sister who raised her after her mother died of tuberculosis. Eduarda herself had lost her own mother in her childhood; the narrator's mother had been Eduarda's teenage friend. Eduarda's father, then in his fifties, falls in love with the young girl and marries her. The December-May romance is one previously seen in Quiroga's works, as is the theme of the orphan. In *The Young Plácida,* however, no less than four characters lose their mothers in early childhood or infancy: Eduarda, the narrator, Plácida, and Plácida's infant daughter. The tragedy is obviously one with which Quiroga herself identifies closely, and the repetition of the situation within the short novel explains in part the narrator's intense interest in the unknown, dead young woman.

Plácida's father was murdered when she was still a small infant. Neighbors assumed responsibility for the orphan, passing her around from home to home. In a sense she belonged to the whole village and yet to no one. From childhood on, she understood that she had to work to pay for her keep. Thus the narrator suggests that Plácida was never young; only in death does she acquire a look of beauty or youth. Nothing ever belongs to Plácida until she becomes pregnant and the neighbors help build a humble little house for her and Salvador. The narrator conjectures that the unborn child and the hut are the only things to which Plácida might ever have attached the possessive "my" (*P,* 55). The narrator knows that Plácida was several months pregnant before she and Salvador were married, and she imagines how he might have courted her, treating her in the same way that he might have used an animal, and she responding with the humble subservience expected of women (*P,* 57–58). To support his young wife and their future child, Salvador is forced to go to sea, as are many Galician men, and is gone when Plácida dies. Her only tie with him in the final months is a phone call.

Only when she is in labor and the baby does not come immediately does Plácida call for help. The peasant women come, bringing a midwife with them. The birth goes well, but when Plácida becomes pale, they send for a practitioner who in turns sends for the doctor. By that time it is too late, for Plácida has been hemorrhaging. The doctor's anger and the narrator's comment indicate that the poor peasants do not normally seek medical care unless a life is in danger. The narrator's sense of rebellion at the senseless death of a young woman is not shared by the peasant women, who tend to accept and forget: "They have accepted time while I rebel, because I think. They don't have time to think, or perhaps they think as cows ruminate, unconsciously, at the edge of the meadows. Because sometimes I am surprised at the naked truth — the beautiful and terrifying absolute face of truth — that comes from their mouths, in a natural way, as they lift their children in their arms" (*P,* 59).

Among the most successful scenes in the short novel are those treating Salvador's telephone calls. In the first chapter, Juana, the local telephone operator, recounts Salvador's last call to Plácida. Quiroga describes quite vividly the nervousness Plácida feels at expecting a phone call and the difficulty she has in talking to her husband, an attitude one might well expect from a woman who has never used a telephone before. After Plácida has died, no one in the village wants to break the news to Salvador. When he calls again, Juana blurts the truth out to him. "Is Plácida there?" he asks. "No," replies Juana. "She's in the ground" (*P,* 63). The narrator tries to imagine how Salvador must have reacted to the tragic news. She feels that only she could really describe to him the pathos of Plácida's death but that when he finally comes home, even she will not want to tell him.

In *The Young Plácida* Quiroga describes with deep emotion the tragedy of one individual's life and death. The technique is highly subjective, the narration being almost entirely the personal reaction of one person to the situation. At moments the style is lyric, particularly when the narrator describes the October beauty of Galicia or expresses her religious feeling when faced with death. Always present in the background, however, is a realistic view of the Galician peasant, his poverty and suffering, his ignorance and his stoicism.

CHAPTER 4

The Experimental Novels

THERE is a noticeable evolution in the narrative technique of
Elena Quiroga from her first novel to *Something's Happening
in the Street* five years later. Her first effort, *Sonorous Solitude,*
written from the perspective of an omniscient narrator in the third
person, offered little if any internal development of character. The
second novel continued the traditional narrator in the third person
but, because of the *tempo lento* of *Northwind,* allowed the reader
to perceive development of character more effectively. In *Blood*
Quiroga developed character once again externally, but moved to a
more objective narration because of the limited perspective of the
chestnut tree. Her next work chronologically, the short novel *Bus
One,* moved even closer to the objective realism that dominated the
Spanish narrative of the 1950s, but with some possibility for internal development of character via the interior monologues of the
passengers on the bus. Finally, in the second short novel, *The Other
City,* Quiroga shifted almost entirely from external narration to
internal, giving us the inner thoughts of various characters through
utilization of a multiperspective technique. The structural devices
present in *The Other City* — multiple perspective, interior monologue, flashback, and stream of consciousness — are the same ones
which she was to use in *Something's Happening in the Street,* the
novel generally recognized as being the first of her innovative
works.[1]

I Something's Happening in the Street

Like the two short novels that preceded it, *Algo pasa en la calle
(Something's Happening in the Street)* takes place in Madrid. As
the action of the novel begins, Ventura, a college professor, has just
died as the result of a fall when the balcony on which he was lean-

ing gave way. The old house in which he lived with Presencia, his second wife, is located on a nonexistent street near the geographically real Cuesta de la Vega. Although the city is of less importance in this novel than in *Bus One,* Quiroga carefully evokes the atmosphere of this area of Madrid, along with the nearby Plaza de Oriente, Bailén, and the viaduct. The author states that the accident is not based on any particular episode, although many older structures in the city pose hazards of this nature, and that she deliberately made up a street name so that readers would not feel that she was writing of a real situation.[2]

Central to the novel is the theme of divorce, relatively unusual in the Spanish novel for, with the exception of the years of the Second Republic (1931–1936), Spain has had no divorce, only legal separation. Quiroga takes advantage of the divorce reform of the 1930s to create the basic situation in her novel. Ventura, an idealistic, intellectual man, had been married to Esperanza, a wealthy woman more interested in materialistic concerns and her social life than in Ventura's work. In spite of his deep love for their little daughter Agata, Ventura decides to seek a divorce. Later, after the Civil War, he meets Presencia, one of his young students. They become lovers, and when he learns that she is pregnant, he marries her in a civil ceremony; they have one son, Asís, legally born out of wedlock. As a result of Ventura's death, these characters, along with Froilán, Agata's husband, are brought together for the first time. Because the Catholic church and Spanish society do not recognize either Ventura's divorce or his civil marriage to Presencia, she has been ostracized by their neighbors. The adolescent Asís, only recently told by schoolmates of his father's first marriage, now views himself as illegitimate. Quiroga is interested in the impact that the broken marriage has had on all of the people involved, particularly Agata, but because of Spanish laws, the psychological and sociological implications are far greater than they might have been in a non-Catholic country.[3]

Through the memories of Presencia and Esperanza, as well as the sympathetic analysis of Froilán, who had never met Ventura but who tends to identify with him, we learn that Ventura suffered greatly at losing his daughter. Initially the child was told by her mother that her father was dead; later, learning that this was not true she felt doubly betrayed: her father had abandoned her and her mother had lied to her.[4] But Ventura had never stopped loving

Agata; he always carried with him the newspaper clippings of her marriage and of the birth of her twin daughters. It is his personal tragedy that he was forced by Esperanza to be permanently separated from his child. In marrying Presencia, he has also been forced into sacrificing his sincere religion. In spite of his inner anguish, however, it is clear that Ventura loves Presencia and that they have been very happy together during the fifteen years of their marriage. It is also clear that Presencia, although not religious, is anything but the *femme fatale* that Esperanza has believed her to be. At thirty-six, she is slender and inconspicuous; Froilán finds it difficult to believe that she is that old or even that she is a mother.

In *Something's Happening in the Street,* Quiroga intended to show societal reaction to divorce or separation and civil remarriage in Spain. It is interesting to note, therefore, to what extent Spanish critics misinterpreted the reality of the situation described and tended to see the novel from the same viewpoint as Esperanza. Several of them suggest that the novel deals with adultery and that Asís is illegitimate.[5] Others believe that Ventura committed suicide, an idea that even Esperanza rejects as implausible (*SH,* 33).[6] One critic, apparently wishing to establish that this is a Catholic novel, erroneously asserts that in the final pages Presencia is converted.[7] In fact, Presencia calls a priest when she knows that Ventura is dying and then leaves the room so that he may renounce their "sinful" marriage and die with the blessing of the church; but she herself is incapable of seeking refuge in religious faith.

Quiroga's skill as a psychological novelist is particularly apparent in *Something's Happening in the Street.* Because of her multiperspective technique, she is able to develop internally the characters of Presencia, Esperanza, Agata, Asís, and Froilán. Through flashbacks in the perspectives of the two wives, we are also given Ventura's own words, allowing a more thorough view of him than would be received merely by the comments of other characters. Except for a few short passages where an omniscient narrator inexplicably intervenes, throughout the novel the reader is allowed to reach his or her own opinion of the situation and the people involved. While it is quite clear that the bias is in favor of Ventura in the Ventura-Esperanza conflict and that Esperanza is the least likeable of the characters — a vehicle for a certain limited criticism of the hypocrisy of the upper social classes — Quiroga does not create the diametrically opposed husband and wife that Delibes later presented in *Five Hours with Mario*. The comparison of these two novels has been a repeated subject of critical attention.[8] As Janet Winecoff Díaz has pointed out, it is unlikely that Delibes was unfamiliar with Quiroga's novel and, although he did not merely imitate the earlier novel, there are a number of obvious similarities.[9] The most notable of these are the death of the husband prior to the beginning of the novel and the contrast between the scholarly, idealistic man and the materialistic, self-centered woman. However, there are also a number of important differences between the two works. Delibes writes almost the entire novel in a stream-of-consciousness style reflecting only the perspective of the wife, and his characters are more one-sided and stereotypical. Unlike Delibes' Carmen, Quiroga's Esperanza is not totally despicable. Even Froilán, who identifies closely with the dead man, feels that he should not betray her trust, and Agata, with her own raised consciousness after her father's death, realizes that under Esperanza's happy façade of parties and trips lies a sad and lonely woman. Because of Quiroga's more complex novelistic structure, we are given several viewpoints about each of the principal characters, viewpoints that are not necessarily in agreement but which collectively allow us to reach a more thorough understanding of the person's true nature.

Entrambasaguas attributes the success of *Something's Happening in the Street* in large part to Quiroga's decision to begin the novel's action after Ventura's death.[10] Had she related the events in chronological order, the accident coming at the end would inevitably have seemed melodramatic, as does the death at the end of *Northwind*. Critics have noted that the technique is not unique to Quiroga. Díaz cites the example in Chile of María Luisa Bombal's *La amortajada* (*The Woman in a Shroud*, 1941).[11] Sobejano mentions two novels in Spain that appeared at the same time or shortly after *Something's Happening in the Street:* Ignacio Aldecoa's *El fulgor y la sangre* (*Splendor and Blood*, 1954) and Juan Goytisolo's *Duelo en el Paraíso* (*Mourning in Paradise*, 1955); he suggests that Faulkner is the common source for all three novels.[12] Specifically Faulkner's *As I Lay Dying* (1930) introduces both a dying or deceased character as the pivotal figure and a multiperspective technique.

Something's Happening in the Street is also related to Faulkner in its fluidity of time. The external time of the novel is relatively

short, perhaps eight hours from the arrival of Esperanza and
Froilán at Ventura's house to 4:00 P.M. when the funeral procession
leaves with Ventura's body. At intervals throughout the novel,
Quiroga indicates exactly this external time, noting that it is 10:00
A.M., that Asís' train arrives at 11:00 A.M., etc. The internal,
subjective time of the various characters, however, spans a period
of almost thirty years. In their thoughts the characters do not pinpoint the moment from the past that they are reliving, but a careful
reading makes it possible to determine the approximate year because of the references to the Civil War and to the ages of the
characters. The present is undoubtedly 1954; Ventura married
Presencia fifteen years earlier, following the Civil War, at a time
when he was temporarily the victim of political reprisals. Presencia
is thirty-six; her childhood memories therefore date from the late
1920s. There is a constant flow from present to past to present
throughout the novel, with the moments from the past presented
out of chronological sequence. Esperanza, for example, recalls first
her recent experience at being awakened by the phone call announc-
ing Ventura's death (Chapter I). Then, in a flashback, she evokes
the period immediately following her separation from Ventura
(Chapter II). Moving farther backward in time, she thinks of the
conflicts she and Ventura had before the separation (Chapter III).
Similarly, in Presencia's thoughts the past is revealed to us in fragmentary fashion. The first time we are given Presencia's perspective, she evokes the preceding day and her own happy mood prior
to Ventura's tragic accident (Chapter V). Somewhat later, her
thoughts shift to the time of her marriage, back to her childhood,
and then again to Asís' childhood (Chapter VII). Only near the end
of the novel does Presencia evoke the time when she first met Ventura (Chapter XVI).

Quiroga makes skillful use of a number of structural devices to
give unity to her narration in spite of the constant shifts in time and
perspective. The change from one level to another, for example,
may be prompted by a particular action or sensory perception. The
smell of the acacia that Presencia has placed by the open coffin,
much to the shock and dismay of Esperanza, jolts Esperanza back
to the present from her reveries (*SH,* 31). When Presencia gives to
Froilán the newspaper clippings of Agata that her husband has always carried with him (Chapter VI), this causes her to remember
her husband's anguish at losing Agata and their experience of

seeing Agata at a puppet show in the Retiro (Chapter VII). Presencia's memories of strolls with Ventura in the sunny streets of Madrid (Chapter XII) bring her back to the sunlit room where his body lies (Chapter XIII). Similarly, the various perspectives may be linked by the contrapuntal device of having one voice repeat a theme introduced by another. In Chapter I, Froilán evokes a conversation with Agata in which she accuses him of defending Ventura because all men stick together (*SH,* 17). In the following chapter Esperanza evokes a conversation with Uncle Fermín in which she makes the same accusation (*SH,* 29). Esperanza uses Uncle Fermín as a source of information on Ventura's activities following their divorce. When Agata learns that her father is alive, she resorts to Uncle Fermín in exactly the same way (Chapter XIV). Early in the novel, Presencia ponders the possible meaning Ventura intended when he once said that someday they would free themselves of him (*SH,* 63). Later Esperanza has related thoughts when her friend Reyes says that she is now free of Ventura (*SH,* 197). More commonly, however, the ties between the various perspectives are provided by having two or more characters evoke the same situation from the past. For example, Esperanza's decision to lie to Agata by telling her that her father is dead is reviewed from the perspectives of Esperanza, Presencia, Froilán, and Agata.

In most of the novel Quiroga develops only one level of consciousness at a time, that is, one character's perspective either in the present or the past. On several occasions, however, she skillfully juxtaposes two levels in the same scene. Such is the case in Chapter IX, when Esperanza and Froilán stop for coffee on their return from seeing Ventura's body. The two discuss Agata's childhood and, as they do so, we are given a counterpoint between Esperanza's spoken words and Froilán's inner thoughts. In Chapter XVII, two examples of this technique occur. During her phone conversation with Reyes, Esperanza's thoughts drift to the past, including passages in which Ventura speaks in his own words. Esperanza's interior monologue is simultaneous with the phone conversation in the present. Just as Esperanza hangs up, Agata arrives. The two carry on a conversation in which their dialogue is juxtaposed with both women's inner thoughts about each other.

Also of considerable interest in terms of structure is Quiroga's approach to point of view, for she blends in *Something's Happening in the Street* passages in first, second, and third persons. The introspective passages, reflecting the inner thoughts of the individual characters, may be written in either an indirect third person or the first person. In some cases, such as Agata's thoughts in Chapter XIV, the point of view may shift within a given flashback. As previously indicated, a few passages of the novel are written from the point of view of an omniscient narrator in the third person; these are undoubtedly the least satisfactory sections of the work. The narrator intervenes, for example, in the final paragraph of Chapter II to tell us what Ventura was really like (*SH,* 33) and again in a brief paragraph near the end of the novel to tell us what Asís did not think (*SH,* 212). The consistency of the narrative technique is also broken by the insertion of past scandals in the neighborhood that Presencia never heard about (Chapter XII) and by a poetic digression, written in the first-person plural but by some unspecified narrator, on the visits of neighbors to a home where a death has occurred (Chapter II). These passages, however, are of minor importance in the context of the total novel. Quiroga's most innovative use of point of view in *Something's Happening in the Street* is the introduction of a second person. Later, Esperanza and Agata, while thinking of each other during their conversation, also mentally address one another in the second person. This is, of course, a very normal use of "you" within a narrative, but Quiroga extends the use of "you" in one passage where the narrator addresses the character in the second person. The passage occurs during Esperanza's thoughts about her divorce simultaneous with her phone conversation (*SH,* 199-200). Michel Butor, exponent of the French new novel, is generally given credit for the creation of this use of second person in *La modification* (1957).[13] Obviously, Quiroga's brief use of the technique antedates Butor.

Although *Something's Happening in the Street* is quite different from Quiroga's early works in its structure and technique, the novel is related to her work as a whole through the character of Presencia. Orphaned as a child, Presencia spends her adolescence with her aunt, uncle, and cousins. The aunt exploits her and is jealous when she does better work academically than the woman's own children. Presencia becomes the solitary, taciturn kind of person so frequently depicted by Quiroga. Ventura, almost twenty years her senior, is also an isolated, introverted character. Although the two were meant for each other, as were José and Elisa in *Sonorous Solitude,* there is a barrier of silence between them when it comes to

Ventura's inner anguish. Like Elisa or Marcela, Presencia has difficulty expressing her emotions, and following Ventura's death she is at first unable to cry. At the end of the novel she is left quite alone, having lost the man she loved and knowing that a barrier now exists between herself and her son. Presencia's character and personal situation are repetitive of certain aspects of earlier works, but the psychological development here is handled more convincingly.

The title for Quiroga's novel comes from *Juan de Mairena* by Antonio Machado. In the passage, which Quiroga quotes at the beginning of her work, Machado suggests that "what's happening in the street" is poetic language, thus implying that there is poetry in routine events and colloquial expressions. This is a theory which Quiroga herself clearly endorses. In *Something's Happening in the Street* she has taken an accident, the kind one might casually read about in the daily newspaper, and has explored in depth the dramatic and psychological implications of that accident in the lives of the people it touches.

II   The Sick Woman

At the heart of *La enferma (The Sick Woman)* there is a probing of the psychological response of the various people whose lives have been touched by a tragedy. Liberata, the title character, has been lying in bed with her face to the wall, speaking to no one, for twenty years; her illness began the day she learned that her childhood sweetheart had married someone else. In the small Galician fishing village where Liberata lives, the whole town continues to be preoccupied with her, despite the passage of decades.

Of Quiroga's many characters, Liberata is perhaps the one that seems the least credible. The author notes that a number of critics have made this observation, but that they are wrong in that the character was drawn directly from life.[14] When she was working on *Blood,* Quiroga sought the peace and quiet of Rianjo on the Ría de Arosa where, like the fictitious narrator of *The Sick Woman,* she stayed in Liberata's house. She soon realized that Liberata's story could well be the basis for a novel. At one point in the novel Alida, who has taken care of the sick woman for many years, tells how she celebrated the death of Telmo, Liberata's one-time sweetheart, with champagne, forcing Liberata to drink, too, and then pulled her from her bed to "dance" with her. Baeza has termed this scene exaggerated and incredible,[15] but Quiroga states that the real-life Alida told her it happened. Not all critics, however, rejected the novel as unbelievable; one Galician reviewer noted at the time that *The Sick Woman* was a *roman à clef* and claimed to have been a friend of the real-life Telmo.[16]

In at least one sense, the narrative technique employed in relating the story of Liberata and Telmo resembles the basic structure of *Something's Happening in the Street.* When the action of the novel begins, Telmo has been dead for several years; Liberata cannot or will not speak for herself. As with Ventura in the earlier novel, we can know these characters only through the testimony of others, and that testimony is sometimes contradictory because of the bias of the witnesses. Given that this is Quiroga's intentional perspective, it is surprising that Baeza considers the relative lack of development of these characters to be a defect: "Telmo, even more than Ventura of *Something's Happening in the Street,* is devoid of autonomous life, empty."[17] In fact, Quiroga's technique here is very similar to that of the French new novel that was beginning to emerge at about the same time. The novel is a search, in this case for the meaning behind Liberata's existence, and neither the narrator nor the reader has any prior knowledge of the situation. The narrator remains to some extent anonymous — she has no name, generally being referred to by those in the village as "the stranger." The narrator listens to the perspectives of various characters — the priest Don Simón Pedro, Alida, Alida's niece Lucía, the telephone operator Justa, and Telmo's sister Angustias — and then must form her own opinion on the true character of Liberata. She does not tell the reader precisely what that opinion is, so that the reader, too, must actively participate in the novel. Quiroga herself has little enthusiasm for the French new novel, but all of the above techniques are characteristic of that genre.[18]

Although the title of the novel might indicate otherwise, within *The Sick Woman* Liberata's life actually functions as a story within a story. The unifying force of the total novel and the central figure is the unnamed narrator. The book is divided into two parts, with Chapters XIII–XXV coming after the division. The primary focus of the first part is the narrator, with Liberata's story dominating the second half. Sobejano has stated that the first half deals with the narrator's trip and the second with the various versions of Liberata's case.[19] This is not totally accurate, however, for much of the first part is written in a stream-of-consciousness style and, through the use of flashbacks, tends to emphasize the inner world of the narrator as much as, if not more than, the external world of· her journey, namely, a boat trip to Rianjo and her arrival at the village. Castellet is likewise incorrect when he describes the first half as the evocation of the setting.[20] Castellet finds that the creation of atmosphere in that first part is very well done, but curiously he criticizes the second half, with its various introspective narrations on Liberata and Telmo, as lacking creative process. In their analysis both of these critics are apparently misled by the division of the novel into two parts. Another critic, writing in *La Voz de Galicia,* is far more perceptive when noting that the novel actually contains three stories: the narrator's past, the narrator's present, and Liberata's tale.[21]

The narrator's interest in Liberata develops gradually in the first part of the novel. In the early chapters, during the boat trip, the flow of the narrator's thoughts includes her reason for making the journey — to see for the first time a piece of land her husband has owned for years on the Galician coast before he sells it — and the fact that she will be staying in the home of a relative of his. Chapters I and II, during the boat trip, and Chapter V, when she arrives in the village, are dominated by the narrator's thoughts of her past. Her attention is brought back to the present at the close of Chapter V when she sees Liberata's closed door. In the remaining chapters of the first part, the emphasis on Liberata grows, with the references to the latter intermingled with the narrator's own preoccupation with herself, with her husband's past, and with the village. In Chapter VI, Alida talks of Liberata's dead mother and of her two brothers, both of whom have left Spain; one of them is a businessman in Argentina and the other, a professor in the United States. In Chapters VII, VIII, and IX, the narrator meets Don Simón Pedro, who comes to the house and talks to her of Liberata and Telmo's childhood; interspersed in this conversation are the narrator's thoughts of her husband Víctor and her reaction upon first entering Liberata's room — an event which actually takes place after the conversation with the priest. In Chapters X and XI, Justa tells the narrator about Liberata, Telmo, and Angustias, who lives upstairs from the telephone operator; this conversation, too, is intermingled with the narrator's personal thoughts. In the final chapter of the first part the narrator finally visits the beach that she has always considered something of a secret love from her husband's past. The trip to the beach had been postponed for several days because of the weather; the narrator has now accomplished her purpose in coming to the village.

From this analysis of the first part, it is quite clear that the narrator herself, her trip, and her reaction to Rianjo form the primary focus of these chapters, but that Liberata's case increasingly attracts the attention of narrator and reader alike. In the second part, Liberata's story dominates in ten of the chapters, with the final three chapters of the novel reverting to the narrator and her stream of thoughts. With the shift in focus in Chapters XIII-XXII there is a concommitant shift in point of view. The first part of the novel and the final three chapters are written in the first person from the perspective of the narrator; the conversation of the other characters is presented us through the thoughts of the narrator. The first ten chapters of the second half, however, are primarily monologues by the various other characters without intervention from the narrator. In Chapters XIII and XIV, we hear Don Simón Pedro speak. Chapter XV is the voice of Lucía, who gives us her viewpoint of Alida and Dámaso, Alida's husband; Lucía feels that her aunt treats her like a servant and that there is something indecent about the Alida-Dámaso-Liberata relationship. In Chapters XVI, XVII, and XVIII, Alida angrily rejects Lucía's accusations, which she has overheard, and speaks at greater length of Liberata's tragedy. Throughout these chapters the narrator remains silent; only from the context of the comments may we know who is speaking to her. In Chapter XIX, Dámaso comes to the stranger, at his wife's request, to defend himself from Lucía's accusations; he says very little about Liberata, and is interrupted by Justa's nephew, who comes to tell the narrator that she has a phone call.

Quiroga uses the phone call as a mechanism to expose the narrator to the testimony of two more witnesses, neither of whom would logically come to see her at Liberata's house. Chapter XX gives us the perspective of Justa on the Liberata-Telmo story, while Chapters XXI and XXII are Angustias' defense of her brother. The phone call from Víctor also serves to bring the narrator's attention back to herself and to prompt her decision to return to her home in Madrid. The final chapters, like the early chapters of the novel, give us her thoughts while traveling and immediately upon her arrival at her destination.

Although Entrambasaguas has declared that *The Sick Woman* is technically perfect,[22] not all critics have shared this opinion, particularly in view of the division of the novel into two parts with predominantly different points of view and narrative focus. As was the case with *Something's Happening in the Street,* some negative criticism may be explained by the time period in which Quiroga wrote the work. Many critics were simply not prepared for a novel with shifting points of view or for the stream-of-consciousness style. Quiroga was again somewhat ahead of the times, even somewhat ahead of the development of the *nouveau roman* in France. Surely Castellet is wrong when he states that the juxtaposition of various perspectives involves no creative process on the author's part. Even a critic as astute as Arturo Torres Ríoseco has difficulty with this multiperspective technique: "It is a shame that the constant change of narrators and the different levels in the narrative often confuse the reader and weaken this bitter and bold novel."[23] Delano, obviously an admirer of Quiroga in general, similarly fails to understand the stream-of-consciousness style of the early chapters: "The technique of the interior monologues along with the flashbacks is at times distracting and annoying, often to the extent that the narrator's thoughts clutter up the story, causing an unnecessary interruption."[24] Although *The Sick Woman* is actually less complex in structure and presents fewer stylistic difficulties than either the novel that immediately preceded it or *The Mask*, which followed, some critics at least were not ready to accept Quiroga's narrative techniques. The criticism that the unity of the novel is disrupted by the radical shift in perspective from the first part to the second part is, of course, a more valid one than the points cited above. If one views the novel as Liberata's story, the shift in narrative focus does, indeed, seem to be a defective device. This may well be Delano's viewpoint, too, and would explain her feeling that the "narrator's thoughts clutter up the story" in the first part. However, if one views the total novel not as Liberata's story but rather as the narrator's, with Liberata's case forming a story within a story, then the overall structure of the novel begins to fall into place.

Quiroga prepares for the shift in narrative perspective in the beginning of the second half in two ways. On one level we know what the narrator's situation is in the little town. She has been there long enough that people are willing to talk to her at length; her presence in Rianjo has taken on such importance in a village that has few visitors from the outside that we can also understand why each person is eager to have "the stranger" hear his or her side of the story. More important, however, is the development within the narrator. The narrator gradually begins to shift her thoughts from herself to the sick woman. Following her trip to the beach, she has temporarily found some inner peace; she is forty-three years old, childless, somewhat frustrated by her existence, but momentarily willing to accept her role in life. Her description of her walk back to town from her husband's property is filled with symbolism: "I am on a flat area before beginning the descent by the shore. My whole being is on a plain. There were roads that I climbed with happiness, shouting into the wind. Now I am on the plain and peace is slender, gray, serene. At the cemetery gate I cross myself. It's my turn to descend."[25] Were she not now preoccupied with Liberata, there would be no reason for her to remain in Rianjo. In fact, her husband's phone call at the end of Chapter XIX is prompted by his concern that she has not announced her return to Madrid. The narrator's interest is not mere curiosity; something in the sick woman's being has struck a responsive chord in her, making her identify with Liberata: "I looked at that face avidly, as if the mask of life, of human beauty, of woman — not individual, but generically — was being revealed to me. And at the same time, something hidden within me was unfolded there. The very beautiful head of that woman seemed like a mirror that was held out to me and I saw there, beyond my face, the boundless suffering of a poor woman — my suffering or that of the human race" (*E*, 80–81). Thus, in the first ten chapters of the second part, the narrator stills the flow of her own thoughts to listen carefully to the monologues about Liberata in hopes of learning not only the truth about the sick woman but the truth about herself and perhaps about women in general.

The relationship between the narrator and Liberata has been observed by several critics. Sobejano, for example, quite correctly states that "Liberata, finally, comes to symbolize the restrained and hidden double of the barren and unsatisfied visitor."[26] The precise form and meaning of this sense of identification on the part of the narrator is never explicitly given in the novel. Fernández Almagro, in a favorable review of *The Sick Woman,* considered this a defect, suggesting that the psychological tie between Liberata and the stranger should have been better developed.[27] However, it is difficult to imagine how Quiroga might have explained the tie more fully without damaging the novel. The only character in a position to develop the parallel is the narrator herself, and her sense of identification with Liberata is far more intuitive than intellectual. At the close of the novel she attempts to explain to Víctor how she and Liberata are alike, and he laughs (*E*, 238). He can think of similarities only in physical terms, and the narrator does not share Liberata's beauty. The narrator then renounces any hope of explaining to him the inner similarities, and, of course, there is no need for her to explain them to herself. As would be the case with the *nouveau roman*, the reader must participate actively in the novel, attempting to enter the narrator's consciousness and perceive reality as she does.

In one sense *The Sick Woman* is closely related to *Profound Present*, which Quiroga was to write almost twenty years later. In the latter work the author juxtaposes the lives of two very different women, both of whom commit suicide, and establishes that, as different as their life-styles were, neither had anything to live for. In *The Sick Woman* the narrator and Liberata share the realization that their lives are empty and meaningless. Whether Liberata really went mad when she saw Telmo get off the boat with his bride or whether, like Pirandello's Henry IV, she merely feigns the madness to avenge herself at Telmo's expense, is never really clarified in the novel. Either way, she has renounced freedom and accepted solitude as her way of life. The narrator concludes that this is the only correct approach to either freedom or solitude (*E*, 219). At the end of the novel, when her husband invites a group of friends to celebrate the narrator's return, she finds that she is as lonely in that crowd as Liberata would be in the solitude of her bedroom. Quiroga's interest in the masks that people wear to cover their real feelings, a dominant theme of her next novel, is also apparent in *The Sick Woman*. Liberata's face is now a motionless mask, but other characters, too, hide behind masks. Víctor wears a mask of irony and sarcasm that the narrator would like to tear away (*E*, 219). At the party in the final pages of the novel, the narrator horrifies herself when she tells her friends the details of the personal stories she has uncovered in Rianjo. That she tells these stories in a lighthearted manner is, of course, a way of covering up her own deep involvement in the life of the Galician village. Within herself the narrator feels that her existence has been as barren as Liberata's and that she has lost Víctor, much as Liberata lost Telmo.

Telmo, several years older than the beautiful Liberata, had hopes of becoming a great poet. His family had encouraged him in his dream, perhaps far beyond his real abilities, as Don Simón Pedro now suspects when looking back on the story. Both children had been pampered and humored by their families. Although Liberata was younger than Telmo, it was she who dominated him. Angustias claims that Telmo did establish himself as a writer in Argentina, where he went when his wife after Liberata became ill, but it is more likely true that he failed as a poet and died in poverty as the other people in the village tell the narrator. The narrator's husband, like Telmo, is several years older than she and was dominated by her, even in childhood. Also idealistic, Víctor is an architect who once had grandiose plans for designing cathedrals and beautiful communities. As his illusions were shattered over the years, he turned to alcohol and irony. The youthful dreamer that the narrator married is just as dead as Telmo. The narrator surely senses not only the parallel between her frustrated dreams and Liberata's but also between Víctor and Telmo. When she first arrives in Rianjo, the narrator writes Víctor a despairing letter; she wants him to know that she is still capable of feeling love, pain, and nostalgia, and therefore, she still exists (*E,* 89). But Liberata, too, exists, and she has gone beyond suffering to nothingness (*E,* 81). Meeting Liberata, then, is for the narrator something of an existential experience in which she becomes aware of the absurdity of life.

Although Liberata as a child and as a young woman had always felt herself isolated from others, set apart by her beauty and her social class, when she is betrayed by Telmo the other women in the village tend to empathize with her. But Liberata's madness is such a cross for Telmo to bear that he never recovers from his sense of guilt; in this way, Liberata triumphs. The theme of the jilted sweetheart is a frequent one in Spanish literature,[28] but Quiroga's intention here is not simply to make one more statement on the subject. In their retrospective monologues the various characters probe Liberata's psyche to determine why she reacted as she did to Telmo's betrayal; they do not accept it simply as the normal reaction of an abandoned woman. Moreover, Quiroga links together the destinies of all women, whether or not they marry. The narrator, Angustias, Justa, and Alida all have been frustrated in fulfilling themselves, one way or another. Lucía is not likely to escape this pattern. The wives of the fishermen lead a hard life and age prematurely. The narrator at forty-three looks like a young girl to them, but she, too, knows that youth has slipped away. She projects her own sense of loss at not having children toward the other women, finding that Alida, also childless, releases her maternal instinct on Liberata, but that Justa, who is single and probably should have been a nun, is unhappy at finding herself caring for her nephew. This leads the narrator to wonder if she herself would be able to adapt to caring for a child if she had to. But perhaps the saddest life of all is that of Angustias, who spends her time defending her dead brother and protecting herself from the reality of his life and death. None of the characters in *The Sick Woman* is happy — even the priest, now old and almost blind, had had youthful ambitions never fulfilled. The narrator recalls that Víctor many years before had said that happiness, if it had color, would be gray, and that to be happy was simply to live each moment for itself (*E*, 23). Unfortunately, neither Víctor nor the others have been able to adapt their lives to such a philosophy.

There are aspects of *The Sick Woman* that tie this work to other novels by Quiroga. The narrator is, once again, a solitary person who has trouble communicating her feelings to others, a problem shared by most of the other characters. As a child, the narrator had been teased by her older brothers; the experiences she evokes from her childhood are related to those of Elisa or Tadea. Again, Quiroga alludes to the Civil War and its effect on village life and on the narrator. Of particular interest in the novel are Quiroga's skillful handling of the stream-of-consciousness passages in the early chapters and her vivid descriptions of the boat ride, of life in the fishing village, of the plane ride from Galicia to Madrid, and of the automobile ride from the airport home.

Sigüenza, who correctly identified *The Sick Woman* as being a *roman à clef*, has suggested that the novel has another level of meaning, symbolic of Galicia itself.[29] He sees Liberata, lying with her face to the wall, as symbolizing his region, which has turned its back on Spain. As Liberata escapes from reality, so do other characters escape from their problems by fleeing to the Americas. This, according to Sigüenza, is precisely Galicia's problem, and the symbolic representation of it in *The Sick Woman* makes Quiroga an important regional novelist. Whether or not Quiroga intended such a message in the novel, most readers will tend to view the work on a more universal plane. The contrast between city and village, between the narrator's life and that of those who surround Liberata, is vital to the appreciation of the novel, but this effect might have been achieved by describing any isolated little town and any metropolitan center.

III   The Mask

Like *The Sick Woman, La careta (The Mask)* has two geographic foci: Galicia and Madrid. Moisés, central figure of the novel, is attending a family reunion in Madrid. During the course of the evening, his thoughts frequently revert to the past, sometimes to his adolescence and youth in Vigo, and eventually farther back in time to his childhood in Madrid. Although Quiroga is quite precise in fixing the section of Madrid where the family has gathered in the present and where Moisés lived as a child, she places still greater emphasis on evoking the atmosphere of Vigo. Through Moisés' thoughts, the reader may envision that busy little port city, its hills and waterfront, as well as the house and garden where Moisés lived with his aunt Germana after his parents were killed in Madrid at the beginning of the Civil War. As is true throughout her work, Quiroga carefully develops olfactory images; in the case of Vigo, it is the smell of the sea that frequently rises to Moisés' consciousness. Although the theme is not so important here as in *The Sick Woman,* Quiroga does mention the life of the Galician fishermen. She also presents again the Galician emigration. Moisés is having supper with his six cousins; their father, his maternal uncle Gabriel, remains in Argentina, where he has lived since before the Civil War. The oldest of the cousins, Gabriel, is a sailor, as were other characters in Quiroga's earlier novels: José in *Sonorous Solitude,* Amador in *Blood,* Plácida's husband in *The Young Plácida.*

The geographical background in *The Mask,* however, is very much secondary to the psychological situation of Moisés. Like the beginning chapters of *The Sick Woman,* this novel is written in a stream-of-consciousness style. Unlike *The Sick Woman,* in *The Mask* Quiroga retains one style almost unbroken throughout the seventeen chapters. While the narrator of the earlier novel was interested in the conversations of others so that their words interrupted her thoughts, Moisés pays little attention to the talk at the dinner table. Moisés himself seldom speaks; only in the fourteenth chapter, when he decides to insult his host, Bernardo, does he utter more than a brief phrase. But Moisés also does not listen. He is conscious only of snatches of conversation, which then prompt him to relive moments in the past.

Quiroga sets the passages from the past in italics as an aid to the reader, but Moisés thoughts are rambling, moving sometimes freely from the recent past to a more distant past with no line of demarcation. The reader must be thoroughly immersed in the novel to comprehend; in 1955, when the novel appeared, few Spanish readers or critics were able to handle the complexities of the work. J. L. Cano found it to be "too confusing,"[30] and Alborg declared that Quiroga had gone too far, that the reading was too difficult.[31] Even many critics who praised the novel failed to understand what had really happened to Moisés to make him what he is.

The action of the novel in the present is contemporaneous with the time when it was published, the mid-1950s. External time is brief: from supper of one evening until the predawn hours of the following morning. Subjective time, however, covers a twenty-year period, going back to the outbreak of the Civil War when Moisés was a child of twelve. His father, a military officer of the Nationalist army, had been caught in Madrid, then held by the Republicans, hiding in his own home — an apartment in Madrid on the street Claudio Coello. Whenever the enemy comes to search the house, he takes refuge in a closet, and his wife pushes a wardrobe in front of the door. With the help of the boy, who has orders to play calmly as if nothing were wrong, the mother deceives the men time after time. During this period, the young boy undergoes a difficult emotional experience. He is disturbed that his brave father hides like a coward, a feeling enhanced by his father's deteriorating appearance and obvious fear. When he sees his parents kissing, he is also torn by feelings of jealousy: a full-blown Oedipus complex. Quiroga does not say, but one may assume, that the father's military career had often taken him away from home, so that the child had been closer to his mother to begin with and had probably tended to idealize the distant father. In any event, he comes to feel isolated from his parents and finds himself fraught by feelings that he cannot handle.

For a while the danger subsides, the enemy being convinced that Moisés' father was indeed in Segovia and therefore has long since crossed the line. Then, quite suddenly, the men come back. They know precisely where the father is hiding. Someone has betrayed him. The child sees his father emerge from his hiding place and sees the men's guns. He runs and hides. He hears shots. When he is sure that the men are gone, he comes out. His father is dead, but his wounded mother is trying to call the neighbors for help. Moisés fears that his mother's calls will bring the men back and that he, too, will be killed. He covers her mouth to still her voice and in effect smothers her. When neighbors do come, they believe that the child had tried to save his mother, not realizing that she bled to death because of his action. The rumor is started that the boy is a hero, a story that warps all of Moisés' life. A neighbor from a leftist family takes Moisés with her and her children to France, and later arranges for him to join his aunt in rightist Galicia.

The full expression of Moisés' nightmare, and of his personal guilt, comes in Chapter XVI. Considering how vividly Moisés relives the episode, it is surprising that any readers of the novel failed to note Moisés' role in his mother's death. Yet critic after critic talks of Moisés having witnessed the murder of his parents — something he did not actually do, as he was hiding at the moment of the shots — but not of his guilt.[32] More easily overlooked, however, in an initial reading of the novel is Quiroga's careful preparation for the revelation of Chapter XVI. Moisés at thirty-two is a degenerate; he has squandered the inheritance from his parents, he cannot or will not hold a job, he drinks far too much, and he has corrupted his cousin Agustín. Shabbily dressed, he barely exists on the inheritance left him by his aunt, who carefully set up a trust fund so that he could not get his hands on the capital, only on the interest. Moisés prides himself on his ability to see through the hypocritical masks of other people. Throughout the course of the dinner, he mentally tears away the façade of Bernardo, the respectable businessman; of Ignacia, who hides her sexual exploits to maintain her self-righteous image; of Nieves, the flirtatious little cousin hiding behind a mask of cosmetics; of Flavia, whom Moisés has always loved in his own way but who maintains a happy image in spite of a husband who beats her; of Gabriel, the man of the impeccable uniform. But, as Geneviève McGloin carefully notes in her doctoral dissertation on *The Mask,* the title of the novel also refers to Moisés himself. Over the years Moisés has developed a mask to hide the feelings of guilt that he has never been able to express until finally the mask has become his identity.[33] Because

Moisés has never been able to purge himself of his feelings of guilt or to erase from his mind the death of his parents, the experience is always present in his mind, either at or below the level of consciousness. McGloin is probably quite correct in asserting that the careful reader already knows the details of Moisés' parents' death from the isolated references before the clarification of Chapter XVI.

Moisés' thoughts of the tragedy are triggered by a number of repeated images. In the first page of the novel Moisés imagines what his cousins' reactions would be were he literally to explode with laughter. He imagines the pieces of his body descending over the dining room. And he imagines the unforgettable smell of blood — the smell he himself cannot put out of his mind with respect to the death of his parents. Interspersed throughout the novel are references to blood, to the smell of blood, to wine as a symbol of blood. Another such device, which both tends to give unity to the narrative and to develop Moisés' story is the leitmotiv of hide-and-seek. Frequently in her earlier novels, Quiroga showed children at play; in The Mask, childhood games have a deadly serious meaning. In Chapter II, the cousins in the present refer to how they used to play hide-and-seek at Aunt Germana's. In Chapter III, Moisés returns to the past and relives the games. For him, the fear of hiding, particularly in the dark, was a real one; the issue of someone betraying the hiding place of another child was serious. He deeply admired Flavia, who never seemed to share his fear. Underlying his emotions during the children's game are, of course, his memories of his father and that hiding place. At one point in the flashback to the garden in Vigo he hears a voice saying, "He hasn't done anything. For God's sake. . . . Have mercy."[34] McGloin is quite correct in observing that this is not the voice of one of the cousins at play but rather a return to the moment in Madrid when Moisés' mother had pleaded with the men to spare her husband.[35] Within the passages from the past, Moisés' memories often rise to the surface, just as within the present time in the novel the flow of his thoughts moves frequently to the past. In The Mask the author clearly shows a mastery of the subtleties of stream of consciousness.

While The Mask is undoubtedly Quiroga's most difficult novel to date, it is also the one for which the only serious literary analyses are available. In addition to McGloin's thesis, there is the earlier article by Juan Villegas, "Los motivos estructurantes de La careta, de Elena Quiroga."[36] In this relatively short article Villegas makes an admirable study of a number of important aspects of the novel: the significance of the mask, the Oedipus complex, the religious symbolism, Moisés' need for confession, the repetitive use of smells. Villegas errs in his judgment in only two minor aspects: his misinterpretation of a masquerade scene and, in part as a result thereof, his theory that Moisés identifies Agustín with his father and therefore, wishing to hurt him, becomes the lover of Agustín's mistress.

The masquerade game, like hide-and-seek, functions simultaneously at two levels. When Moisés plays with his cousins, he relives over and over the death of his parents. In the second chapter Moisés returns to the day his cousins decide to dress up in old clothes. Although this is a normal and innocent childhood pastime, in the context of the novel the idea of disguise repeats the leitmotiv of the mask. Moisés remains a spectator. To his horror, Agustín puts on boots, a cartridge belt, and ties a red kerchief around his neck. Moisés begins to cry and runs away. Uncle Gabriel, not knowing how to respond, declares that Moisés has won a prize — for his acting; Flavia, however, realizes that Moisés is not playing. Villegas suggests that Agustín evokes the image of Moisés' father; McGloin, on the other hand, is correct in asserting that Agustín evokes the men who killed Moisés' parents.[37] Moisés' father never wore a cartridge belt in the descriptions we have of him, and certainly the red kerchief would more likely have been the symbol of the Communist soldiers who killed him. When Moisés cries and runs away, he is repeating his actions the day the men came for his father. Here, as in many other moments throughout the first chapters of the novel, Quiroga skillfully gives us clues to the real cause of Moisés' psychological problems. Even the smothering of his mother is indicated before Chapter XVI. The words "mother" and "son" constantly distress him, far beyond the impact that losing his mother would have had. He both resents the motherly affection that others receive — Aunt Elizabeth putting her arm around her children, for example — and resists all efforts to show him affection. Aunt Germana, who obviously loves the boy, intuitively understands this and makes no effort to replace his mother. Although Moisés has great difficulty feeling or expressing any kind of love for anyone, he apparently does hold affection for his aunt. When she is dying, slowly and painfully, from cancer, he is tempted to end her suffering. Within this flashback in Chapter VII there is a

clear reference to his mother's death: "(His child's hand on the be-
loved lips, a little gurgle under his hand, the last breath. . . . Amazement. Look at the hand as if it contained another life. . . . Return.
Recede.)" (*C,* 90). Although she does not speak, Moisés knows
that his aunt knows that he has thought of killing her; he covers his
face.

On one level Moisés is reminiscent of Quiroga's frequently repeated taciturn, isolated character. Unable to tell others of his guilt
and grief, he has bottled up his emotions and allowed them to
destroy his life. Villegas holds that the whole novel serves as
Moisés' attempt to confess. Indeed, on several occasions he has
made an effort to bare his soul. As an adolescent he had attempted
to confess to a visiting priest at his school, but the priest had merely
shrugged off the story, saying that Moisés could only have been an
innocent child. A second effort at confession also meets with failure, at first because the priest will not listen — Moisés has obviously been drinking — and then because he rejects Moisés' rambling story as being the product of his alcoholic imagination. On
another occasion, Moisés inadvertently finds himself telling his
story to a prostitute; she offers a sympathetic ear, but he flees from
her. Even to himself Moisés does not consciously relate the whole
story until, in Chapter XVI, he finds himself in front of the house
where he and his parents lived at the time of the tragedy.

As both Villegas and McGloin note, there is a level of religious
symbolism in the novel. Moisés thinks a great deal about Flavia's
deaf and mute son, Manuel, and identifies himself with the child,
who similarly cannot communicate his feelings. Moisés places himself, too, in the Manuel-Christ role on several occasions. When the
uncle declared that Moisés had won a prize, the boy felt that this
was his INRI (Iēsus Nazarēnus, Rex Iūdaeōrum. Jesus of Nazareth,
King of the Jews. Letters placed above Christ's head to mock him.)
(*C,* 35). Moisés envisions the child Manuel as somehow being able
to redeem them because of his purity, but he also imagines himself
as being a redeemer. After the party, when he knows that Agustín is
following him through the deserted streets, he hopes that Agustín
will catch him and kill him. Through his death he will redeem them
all, even Agustín. But in the end neither his inner confession nor his
religious thoughts have any impact. When Agustín attacks him,
Moisés' desire for self-preservation takes hold, and he fights back,
leaving the dead or dying Agustín in the street. It is the same desire

to survive that had surfaced twenty years earlier causing his cowardice and his resultant guilt.

Moisés' alienation also manifests itself in his inability to love. His dismay at becoming aware of the sexual level of love between his parents and his guilt about his mother carry over into his adult years, making it impossible for him to develop a meaningful relationship with any woman. Bernardo introduces him to the houses of prostitution in Vigo when he is still a teenager, and although Moisés returns there frequently, he is unhappy with the experience. He participates in love-play with both Ignacia and Nieves in their adolescence — we can only surmise how far these relationships go — but again without any real feeling of love. It is Flavia's marriage that upsets him, and he somehow expects his cousin to be visibly sullied by the loss of her virginity. His ambivalent feelings about Flavia probably do result, as Villegas and McGloin suggest, from his tendency to identify her with his mother. The situation with Agustín is somewhat different. Of the cousins, he is the one who most admires Moisés for his bravery. That bravery, of course, is a myth; Agustín's admiration thus constantly opens the wound of Moisés' guilt. His response in his youth is to mistreat Augstín — to leave him out of games and make fun of him. As the years go on, he derives pleasure in corrupting Agustín. His most recent, and perhaps most perverse act, has been his open relationship with Choni, Agustín's mistress. It is unlikely that he becomes Choni's lover to deceive Agustín, the father image, in response to his Oedipus complex — Villegas' theory. More likely, given his own inability to love and his sadistic tendencies with respect to Agustín, he simply cannot bear to see Agustín find any happiness. The emphasis on the sexual aspects of Moisés' life thus serves to reinforce our general impression of his psychological state and alienation.[38]

On another level Moisés is representative of the victims of the Civil War. He has been psychologically crippled by that fratricidal conflict. Ten years after the publication of *The Mask,* other Spanish novelists were to begin analyzing the war objectively, showing that no one really won.[39] Quiroga was already aware of the problem. In clarifying the message of the novel to Coindreau, the French translator, she wrote in 1956: "The problem of a human being who survives the war, his own fear, his own cowardice: the true vanquished person is never the one who died."[40] Moisés survived, but he cannot forget. His guilt, of course, only deepens the psychological impact. Having learned once, in a moment of fear, to put his own survival above all else, he later finds it easier to victimize others. In many respects he is related to the characters of Antonio Buero Vallejo's tragedy *El tragaluz* (*The Basement Window,* 1967) or Ana María Matute's novel *La trampa* (*The Trap,* 1969), both of which deal with the aftermath of guilt stemming from the betrayal of a family member during the Civil War. In these situations, it is really irrelevant whether one belonged to the "winning" or the "losing" side.

Quiroga makes this point clear in one brief reference in *The Mask.* At first Moisés had thought his situation unique. Then he was made aware of the parallel between himself and the son of Aunt Germana's part-time maid. The boy's father had been falsely accused of being a Communist and had been assassinated by the rightists in Galicia. For the first time, Moisés feels that he is part of a collective group: "Above all, both were boys who had no desire to play, perhaps did not know how to, nor had any desire to talk about it" (*C,* 138).

Quiroga believes that she is the first novelist within Spain to suggest that atrocities were committed on both sides.[41] It is her feeling in *The Mask,* as elsewhere, not only that those on both sides suffered and caused tragedies, but also that neither side had the monopoly on goodness and virtue. Aunt Germana is surprised to learn that the leftist neighbor from Madrid would help Moisés to cross the line into rightist territory, but Quiroga's purpose is to show that political or religious differences do not wipe out all human compassion. The conservative Galician aunt finds that many of her assumptions about people are, indeed, open to question. The mother of Moisés' cousins, whom Uncle Gabriel met in Argentina, is an English Protestant. As a little boy, Moisés had therefore been told to pray for his cousins' souls. His priest's attitude is surely that of Aunt Germana, too, until she comes to know Aunt Elizabeth and learns that a Protestant can also be a fine person.

However, the character in the novel most inclined to question overtly traditional values and prejudices is Felisa, Gabriel's daughter who has lived with Bernardo and his wife Constanza since the death of her mother. An emancipated young woman, who does as she pleases, Felisa feels that her generation suffers apathy because her parents' generation has given them a land covered with blood and garbage. She calls them the "bridge generation" between the past and youth, but she feels that the bridge itself is without importance: "The important thing is not to be the bridge; it's to be the road that passes under it or the river. Or the land on one side or the other that holds it up, or what goes above it..." (*C*, 161). The older people try to justify their lives by blaming the Civil War. Felisa will not accept the excuse, refusing even to respect Moisés as a victim. It is doubtful that Quiroga herself agrees with all of Felisa's opinions, but her assertions do tend to indicate that not only Moisés, the ne'er-do-well, but Bernardo, the successful businessman, belong to the same generation and that they, as well as Spain's youth in the 1950s, continue to be affected by the Civil War.

In the first ten chapters of the novel, Moisés begins his thoughts in the present and then shifts to the past, with a certain amount of flow between past and present throughout each chapter. Chapter XI is entirely in the past, and Chapter XII, which begins in the past, only briefly shifts to the present. Moisés' introspection is broken at the end of Chapter XII with the sound of a door being slammed. Chapter XIII, which begins with Felisa's entrance, is entirely in the present, as are all of the remaining chapters except the key flashback in Chapter XVI. McGloin feels that Felisa's precipitous arrival is contrived and suggests, among other possibilities, that Quiroga includes the character only because this is a *roman à clef* and the scene actually took place.[42] The author, however, denies that *The Mask* is based on fact;[43] even if it were, Quiroga is too skilled as a novelist to include an extraneous character or scene just to be historically accurate. Felisa's arrival does, in fact, serve several functions within the novelistic structure.

On a realistic level, Felisa's arrival is logical. Earlier in the novel we were told that she lives with her aunt and uncle. Nieves, her husband, and Ignacia have all departed. Felisa's return home at such a late hour confirms what we have already been told of her life-style. Her criticism of the older generation might be anticipated from what we know of her and, as mentioned above, tends to reinforce the social commentary of the novel. In one sense Felisa does voice some of Moisés' unexpressed thoughts on the hypocrisy of his cousins. More importantly, however, she snaps Moisés out of his reverie. The cousins are all parts of his past, and their presence takes him backward in time. Felisa is someone he hardly knows; she represents youth and the present, thus attracting his attention. For the first time during the evening, he listens to the conversation. Superficially, then, the narrative technique seems to have changed, ending the stream of consciousness, but the change reflects Moisés' interest in what is being said. At one point he even starts to break out of his lethargy, to move forward and say something, but Flavia inadvertently pushes him back to silence by assuming that he is going for another drink and advising him, as people have been all evening, not to drink any more. Moisés thus continues in his role as spectator, not intervening either when Gabriel slaps his daughter or when Felisa hurls a final insult at Flavia: "Stay with Moisés" (*C*, 166). Felisa's open hostility and cruelty, as well as Moisés' guilt at having not defended Flavia, serve as the catalyst to Moisés' actions in the following scenes. After Felisa has left and Gabriel has departed, Moisés begins to insult Bernardo, something he has never previously done. He reminds Bernardo, whose marriage with the older, rich, and unattractive Constanza has produced no children, that Bernardo once forced a girl friend into having an abortion. Moisés taunts Bernardo with the fact that now he has no children, much as he has begun earlier in the evening to taunt the drunken Agustín with the thought that Choni is pregnant, but that the child is Moisés', not Agustín's. The violence of Moisés' words with Bernardo thus prepare us for the drunken assault by Agustín in the final pages of the novel.

If we are to fault Quiroga for a break in her narrative technique, the defect comes not so much in Chapter XIII with Felisa's conversation as in Chapter VIII, with an introspective view of Constanza's unhappy youth. The only way this section can belong within Moisés' thoughts is if he is reconstructing Constanza's probable feelings from what Bernardo has confided in him over the years. While this is possible, there is no direct explanation within the novel, and so the scene seems out of place. For the most part Quiroga maintains the stream-of-consciousness style throughout the novel, manipulating skillfully a difficult technique. She does this so well that the reader may fail to grasp the limitations of a narrative that gives us the perspective of only one character. We really never do know what the cousins think of Moisés, only what Moisés thinks that they think. The only basis we have for an objective view is the occasional dialogue. Quiroga places the reader within the consciousness of Moisés, and it is from his perspective alone that we view her novelistic world.

IV   The Last Bullfight

In her next novel Quiroga does not continue the stream-of-consciousness, single-perspective style developed in *The Mask*. *La última corrida (The Last Bullfight)* deals with the lives of three bullfighters and, in some respects, is a return to the multiperspective technique essayed in *Something's Happening in the Street*. As in her other experimental novels, here there is a fluidity of time, but Quiroga no longer provides typographical aids to the reader — italics to set off passages in the past — so that, while the narrative technique requires less participation on the part of the reader than did the presentation of Moisés' thoughts in *The Mask,* the reader must remain actively involved in order to follow the constant shifting from present to past.

The Last Bullfight is Quiroga's only novel not set in one of the parts of Spain with which the author herself is most familiar: Galicia, Madrid, and Santander. Instead, the action takes place in La Mancha; in preparing the work, Quiroga lived briefly in El Viso del Marqués, thus guaranteeing the authenticity of the countryside and little town that she describes. In the final lines of the novel, her words "Solitude and dust"[44] are particularly evocative of this dry, inland region, so different from the green, coastal landscape of Galicia.

More surprising than her ability to create the atmosphere of central Spain, however, is Quiroga's skill at describing the world of the bullfight: the arena, the spectators, the men whose lives revolve around bulls and bullfighting. Some years after *The Last Bullfight* was published, Quiroga was interviewed for the bullfighting magazine *El Ruedo*. The journalist wondered why a person from Galicia, the region in Spain that places the least emphasis on bullfighting, would be interested in the topic. The author explained that she is a fan and, having attended many bullfights over the years throughout Spain, was well prepared to write the novel.[45] As at least one critic has observed, however, *The Last Bullfight* is not really a bullfighting novel; the bulls merely form the background.[46] Quiroga's primary interest is the psychology of her three main figures, Manuel Mayor, Pepe Sánchez, and Carmelo. Her descriptions of the arena or of the village tavern, however vivid and realistic, are subordinate to her analysis of character, as was the description of the fishing village in *The Sick Woman*. In this respect her novel is quite different from Angel María de Lera's narrative of the bull-ring, *Los clarines del miedo (The Clarions of Fear),* also published in 1958.[47]

As was true in *Something's Happening in the Street* and *The Mask,* the external time of *The Last Bullfight* is very short. The novel opens at the arena in Almagro, just as the spectacle is about to begin. It ends, only an hour or two later, when Manuel slips and is injured during the fourth bullfight of the day.[48] Internal, subjective time, on the other hand, spans many years. Pepe's thoughts go back to his childhood, perhaps twenty years earlier. Carmelo, the youngest of the three and performing for the first time as a bull-fighter, retreats only a few years in his thoughts. Manuel, who is in his fifties and had planned to retire from the bullring before, obviously could span more years in his flashbacks than could the younger men, but Quiroga leaves the chronology of the sections in the past deliberately vague so that we cannot date most of the memories. One brief reference to the Civil War would indicate, however, that Manuel, too, goes back at least twenty years in his thoughts.

Although Quiroga does not label parts in the novel, *The Last Bullfight* is divided into three sections, with an extra blank page being used to separate these divisions. The first such section contains ten chapters, nine of which alternate systematically between present and past, the odd-numbered chapters reflecting the present activity in the bullfighting arena. The pattern is broken with the tenth chapter, which also depicts the present. At this point each of the three bullfighters has already faced one bull and there is an intermission before the final three bulls of the day are to be brought out. In the second section of the novel, Quiroga takes advantage of the break in the bullfighting program to introduce ten chapters, all taking place in the past. While the four chapters dealing with the past in the first section are more or less evenly divided among the perspectives of Manuel, Pepe, and Carmelo, the emphasis in this second section is clearly on Manuel. Chapters XI–XIV deal solely with Manuel. In Chapter XV the perspective shifts from Manuel to Carmelo. Two chapters each are devoted exclusively to Carmelo and Pepe, with Chapter XVIII, like Chapter XV, serving to shift the focus from one character to another. All three chapters in the final section, when the intermission is over, are in the present and deal predominantly with Manuel and his unfortunate accident.

Throughout the novel Quiroga maintains the point of view of the narration in the third person. Although this third person sometimes indirectly gives us the thoughts of one of the main characters, many passages, particularly those in the present, are a more objective description of external reality. The novel also contains a much greater amount of dialogue than any of her previous works, except *Bus One*. Quiroga is particularly skillful at capturing the conversation of people attending the bullfight and of customers at Crespo's tavern *La Oliva*. These passages of realistic dialogue and objective descriptions have led various critics to comment on the relationship of *The Last Bullfight* to the current of objective realism in the contemporary Spanish novel. Bartolomé Mostaza suggests that the language is so real that Quiroga might have captured the speech on tape recordings and then selected and transcribed the dialogue.[49] The same comment has frequently been made of Rafael Sánchez Ferlosio's *El Jarama (The Jarama River),* which won the Nadal Prize in 1955; de Nora and Corrales Egea have, in fact, compared Quiroga's technique with that of Sánchez Ferlosio.[50] It is true that both novelists have succeeded in re-creating quite vividly the speech of common people, but it must be noted that Quiroga had already displayed this capacity in *Bus One,* which antedates Sánchez Ferlosio's novel, so that her effort here is not likely an attempt at duplicating his achievement. Moreover, her novel is distinguished from works of objective realism by its stress on the subjective development of character.

The three bullfighters who serve as the central figures of the narrative represent three different approaches to the sport. They are differentiated not only by age and experience, but also by their sensitivities. Carmelo, the beginner, protegé of Manuel, defines these differences. While Pepe is attuned to the spectators and is motivated by their shouts, Manuel's thoughts are not on the arena but rather on the open plains of La Mancha where the bulls roam free. Carmelo, who feels himself to be alone but somehow between Manuel and Pepe, determines that his own ear will be directed within, that he will listen to the sounds of his own being (*U,* 205). The passages from Carmelo's past almost all relate either to his call to be a bullfighter or to his admiration for Manuel. Pepe, the star of the three, has just returned from a triumphant tour of Mexico. In his thoughts we find references to his experiences there and also to his childhood of relative poverty. But most of the emphasis, as previously noted, is on Manuel.

In many respects Manuel is once again Quiroga's silent, introverted character. He is known for being a man of few words, although Carmelo occasionally has the pleasure of hearing him speak
at length on his experiences. Manuel's natural tendency to withdraw from social contact is reinforced by his partial deafness.
While Pepe is the flamboyant, crowd-drawing star, Manuel is an
aloof man whose life is not totally wrapped up in the arena. He
owns land, keeps a flock of sheep, and is more typically a Spanish
peasant than a bullfighter. Like many of Quiroga's characters,
however, he has a deep love of freedom, and the bull for him is a
symbol of freedom: not the bull of the arena, who is already
marked for death, but the majestic animal who runs free in the
fields. It is this bull that Manuel carries within him, as does every
true bullfighter (*U,* 142). Before being talked into going back in the
arena one more time as Carmelo's sponsor, Manuel had given up
bullfighting, feeling something of the emptiness and frustration because of his advancing age that was also reflected in the narrator of
The Sick Woman. His final bullfight has been an outstanding one,
however, arousing enthusiasm in the crowd, until he slips and falls,
thereby being forced to leave the ring without killing his second
bull. The end of his career is certainly marred by this event, and the
novel ends on a sad note as Manuel goes home alone.

Most critics have praised the portrayal of Manuel very highly. De
Nora has called him the most impressive and complete masculine
figure in Quiroga's novelistic gallery.[51] It is interesting to observe
that in *The Last Bullfight* Quiroga has, in fact, written a novel
dominantly about male characters with a background that is dominantly a man's world.[52] There has, however, been a negative reaction to one aspect of Manuel's portrayal. Part of his memories revolve around his love for Prado, a woman of easy virtue. Corrales
Egea, for example, states that in showing an old bullfighter in love
with a prostitute, Quiroga has succumbed to her melodramatic tendency.[53] Actually, with the vague chronology of Manuel's past, it is
not clear at what age he was Prado's lover, although the relationship did continue after his marriage to Clementa. Prado, for
Manuel, is apparently a free spirit; conquering her gives him something of the same masculine feeling that he derives from bullfighting: "to be a man was Prado, and Prado's sarcasm, and Prado's
deceitfulness, and to make her come and to force her" (*U,* 49).

When Manuel begins to feel old, he again associates Prado with bullfighting: "the things of youth. Bulls and Prado, never more" (*U*, 49). It is certainly not Quiroga's intention to suggest that Manuel is unaware that Prado is unfaithful to him. When he pays no attention to comments made at *La Oliva* it may be that he cannot hear them, or it may be that he chooses to ignore them just as he remains detached from most of the small talk of the tavern.

The Last Bullfight is linked to Quiroga's other novels not only by the character of Manuel but also by her unusual use of poetic and sensory images. *The Mask,* for example, begins with the description of the smell of blood, the smell that Moisés cannot erase from his memory. Similarly, the first paragraph of *The Last Bullfight* develops an olfactory image, this time the smell of horses and bulls. Quiroga uses this smell, along with an emphasis on flies and sweat, to evoke the atmosphere of the bullring. Unlike almost all of Quiroga's preceding works, *The Last Bullfight* includes no religious symbolism and no emphasis on the church. If there is some justification in labeling her a Catholic novelist for the themes of despair, penitence, or faith that she develops in *Blood, The Other City, Something's Happening in the Street,* or *The Mask,* the same cannot be said of this novel.

Although Fernández Almagro has suggested that *The Last Bullfight* is perhaps Quiroga's best novel,[54] it is difficult to justify that judgment. Far more accurate is the appraisal of another critic that the novel fails to make the reader experience the characters as real people, fails to reveal to us their human essence, and lacks any real conflict that could form the core of the novel.[55] Quiroga's probing of her characters' pasts here seems to serve no purpose. In *The Sick Woman* we join in the narrator's search to learn the truth about Liberata. In *The Mask* the source of Moisés' anguish is gradually revealed to us. Here there is no mystery about any of the three bullfighters and hence the retreats to the past clarify nothing for us. Nor do they succeed in making the characters live. Pepe is the most stereotypical of the three, but neither Carmelo nor Manuel is really a convincing, living character. Only in the case of Manuel do we have more than one perspective on a character, and even then Manuel remains something of an enigmatic figure. For this reason, although *The Last Bullfight* is intended to be more of a psychological novel than a bullfighting one per se, its appeal is much more restricted than that of several of Quiroga's other novels.

CHAPTER 5

The Tadea Trilogy

IN her first novel, *Sonorous Solitude,* Quiroga introduced the character of Elisa, whose childhood bore some resemblance to the author's own life experiences. Eleven years later, with the publication of her eighth full-length novel, Quiroga returned to essentially that same character and began a series of three novels dealing with the childhood and adolescence of a motherless girl raised by her maternal grandmother and aunt. The Tadea of this trilogy clearly has much in common with Quiroga herself. Both were born in 1921, Tadea in January and Quiroga in October. Both spend part of their childhood in the relative freedom of the father's farm in Galicia and another part in the more repressive atmosphere of the maternal grandmother's home outside Santander. Both attend and then withdraw from a Catholic girls' boarding school. But Quiroga is quick to reject the suggestion that the novels are autobiographical except in a superficial way. Here, as elsewhere in her novelistic work, she feels that she has transformed reality by her creative art. In reference to the Tadea trilogy, she declares, "It was our world as little girls, as adolescents, as young women, not in the anecdote nor in particular personal characteristics but in the setting, in what might have been because it was."[1]

The Tadea novels are Quiroga's own favorite works.[2] They are also among her works that have received the highest critical acclaim.[3] Although Tadea is not intended to be Elena Quiroga herself, there is an unmistakable ring of authenticity about these novels. The author is close enough to the setting, the historical background, and the characters themselves to give them real life. The novels also excel in their structure and style, as is readily apparent upon comparing them with *Sonorous Solitude.* Gone is the melodramatic tendency of that first novel and gone, too, the tendency to develop character externally. While Elisa's childhood and adolescence formed the basis for only one section of that novel, Tadea's experiences from the age of seven through her late teens span three novels, including the seven-hundred-page *I Write Your Name*. This *tempo lento* results in the slow, deliberate development of Tadea's character from within.

I Sadness

At first glance *Tristura (Sadness)*, with its return to the child character type of *Sonorous Solitude*, impressed some critics as being a reversion to the author's earliest style. McGloin, for example, declares that Quiroga "has reverted to her old linear style and more simple plots."[4] The author, however, rejects this criticism, feeling that *Sadness* and *I Write Your Name* represented a step forward, novels in which she could depict "a world of glances, silences, double meanings, gestures, conventional words that hide the unconventional."[5] In fact, from a structural point of view, *Sadness* more closely resembles *The Mask* than it does Quiroga's earliest novels. As in *The Mask, Sadness* is written in the first person, totally from the perspective of one character. Tadea's thoughts, like Moisés', deal with both present and past, with the passages from the past set in italics. It is through the juxtaposition of these two levels of time — Tadea's past at the farm in Galicia and her present with her grandmother, Aunt Concha, and cousins Ana, Odón, and Clota in Santander — that we come to understand the child's anguish. Unlike Moisés, there are no secrets in Tadea's past, however, and, although neither the flashbacks nor Tadea's thoughts in the present follow a strict chronological order, *Sadness* lacks the stylistic complexity of Moisés' stream of consciousness.

McGloin, moreover, is incorrect in asserting that *Sadness* is a return to a "more simple plot," for from *Something's Happening in the Street* on, Quiroga's novels have had little plot. With the exception of *The Mask*, which does have a story to tell in both the past and the present, Quiroga's experimental novels could each be summarized in a line or two. In this respect Quiroga's novels resemble the French new novel, where pattern is substituted for plot.[6] Rather than a return to the traditional novel — best represented in Quiroga's works by *Sonorous Solitude* and *Northwind* — *Sadness* is a continuation of the more innovative novels of the mid-1950s.

Quiroga's use of the past in *Sadness* is dominantly to develop a

counterpoint between past and present. While in her other novels
flashbacks were primarily triggered by a sensory perception in the
present, in *Sadness* the linking device is generally thematic. A storm
in Santander reminds Tadea of one experienced in Galicia. A visit
to the kitchen in her grandmother's house reminds her of her
father's kitchen. A reference that she herself makes to wild horses
or to the lamb she and her brothers had evokes a flashback in which
she relives those scenes. Stories that her grandmother's servants or
Aunt Concha tell about her mother remind Tadea of what Tina, the
woman who raised her on her father's farm, also told about the
dead Raquel. Throughout the juxtaposition of past and present
there is an implied comparison of the two realities and specifically
an awareness on the child's part that the two views are not consistent. For Aunt Concha, life in the country was immoral and her sister was unhappy there; for Tina, Tadea's mother was blissfully
happy and Aunt Concha is an envious hypocrite.

The passages from the present, in addition to their counterpoint
with Tadea's past in Galicia, are written simultaneously on two
levels. Although we are never told that Tadea's experiences in Santander during the two-year span of the novel's action are, in fact,
remembered by an older Tadea, such an implication exists in the
narrative technique. Many of the chapters begin with extensive
descriptions of the grandmother's house and garden or of the city,
descriptions that the child Tadea would not give to us from her perspective as an eight- or nine-year-old. This is particularly true in the
early chapters of the novel, where the conversation of the governess
Suzanne or other characters is interjected within those descriptive
passages. There is also present in these first chapters a sense that
activities Tadea describes are the repeated ones of her years with
Ana, Odón, and Clota, not a particular episode that she is experiencing at the time of her thoughts. These sections, presented
through the more distant perspective of memory, tend to disrupt
the chronological flow of events and give to the narrative the more
rambling sense of a stream-of-consciousness work.

Unlike Ana María Matute's *Primera memoria* (*First Memory*,
1959),[7] where the reader is always aware that the story is related by
the adult Matia recalling her adolescence, Quiroga does not overtly
suggest this technique here. However, the intervention of an older
narrator is quite clear not only in the aspects already mentioned but
also in two masterful passages in which the narrator synthesizes the

repressive environment in which Tadea finds herself as a child. The first of these, beginning on page 27,[8] is a litany of the restrictions placed on little girls: "Don't talk with the servants. Don't go to the kitchen. What do you have to say to Mariano? Stay out of older people's business. Why are you looking? What are you listening to? A little girl does not listen, does not look to the side. Don't you have your cousins to talk to? Play. Your hands should never be idle...." The second passage (*T,* 167) is structured on the word "closed." The narrator emphasizes all of the doors that are closed in the house, and then repeats the word in other contexts to show the total lack of freedom for the child. Voices, air, roads, and even the source of tears are all closed.

Although there is present in the narration a level of reflection and synthesis that could only come from a more mature perspective than that of the child, all events and characters are screened through Tadea's consciousness. In her innocence there are many episodes not fully understood, and they are left for the reader to interpret. It is very clear that a bewildered Tadea still believes that the wise men bring gifts to children when her aunt gives her a cheap little doll and her own daughter a big, expensive one (*T,* 164). The reader, but not the eight-year-old Tadea, understands that the servants have sent her off to sing a suggestive song and interrupt the lovemaking of Mariano and Dora (*T,* 147–54). Again, the reader, but not the nine-year-old Tadea, understands that the older cousin Ana's "headache" is actually her first menstrual period (*T,* 246–47).

The single most important aspect of *Sadness* is the careful psychological development of this child character. Like Elisa in *Sonorous Solitude,* Tadea suffers at the hands of her aunt and cousins, but these characters do not have the melodramatic overtone of stereotypical villains that their counterparts do in the earlier novel. By using the first-person narrative of Tadea, the author indicates that we have the subjective viewpoint of the child only and that we cannot expect an objective, well-rounded portrait of the secondary figures. Quiroga does, however, include enough dialogue that the reader may to some extent validate the perspective of the child. In some cases Tadea overhears conversations which explain to the reader, if not to the child herself, why certain characters treat her as they do. Tina had suggested to Tadea that her aunt Concha was envious of Tadea's parents' happy marriage. Later we

hear an argument between Concha and her husband which reinforces this opinion; it is quite apparent that Concha feels neglected
and suspects her husband of infidelity. Moreover we also learn that
Concha resented her sister for being their parents' favorite daughter. In psychological terms the reader can understand why the unhappy Concha takes out her frustrations on the innocent Tadea.

The criticism of Concha — her hypocrisy, her bigotry, her lack of
charity and compassion — as well as the more general social criticism in the novel is never overtly expressed. Tadea is too young to
verbalize the value judgments that underlie *Sadness*. The author indirectly makes the reader form his or her own conclusion by the use
of several devices. Sometimes a brief remark by one of the servants
will make us aware of the antagonism between the social classes. In
other cases the repetition of an incident or an attitude will bring the
message home; for example, the cousins have obviously been
taught by their mother to look down on anyone poorer than they,
an attitude they reflect in their treatment not only of Tadea but also
of their grandmother's cousin Julia, the niece of one of the servants, and an older woman who comes to oversee their studying.
Quiroga's most frequent device, however, is the skillful juxtaposition of the conflicting words and deeds of one character or the differing attitudes of two characters. Thus Aunt Concha tells Tadea
almost in the same breath that witches do not exist — a criticism of
the Galician superstition that Tadea has heard at her father's home
— and that the Virgin Mary will cry if Tadea crosses her legs — one
of many lies that are part of a Spanish child's rigid upbringing (*T,*
28). We see Ana eavesdropping (*T,* 131) and then Tadea being pun-
ished for listening behind doors (*T,* 132). Aunt Concha assures the
children that they should not be frightened during a storm if they
have a clear conscience, although she herself is visibly afraid (*T,*
88); on the other hand, Julia, who is truly pure of heart, laughs at
the wind and rain (*T,* 93). Aunt Concha hastily fires Mariano and
Dora when she finds out about their love affair, but she arranges
for the pregnant Tomasa to marry her lover because Uncle Juan
likes Tomasa's cooking.

Tadea is clearly the victim both of her aunt's hypocrisy and of
her notions on raising children. The little girl, whose mother died
when she was still a toddler, has been uprooted from all that was
familiar to her — Tina, her brothers, her father, her dog, the Galician countryside — and placed in the restricted urban environment

where even parts of the garden are off limits to the children. She desperately needs affection, but except during Julia's annual winter visit, she receives none. Those who treat her kindly — her grandmother, her uncle Juan, the family priest — are aloof or simply not in real contact with her daily existence. Aunt Concha, who dominates the child's life, has convinced herself, her children, and the servants that Tadea is a bad child who is always responsible for whatever mischief the children get into. Ana, Odón, and Clota have learned to pretend obedience; in their mother's presence they behave like little angels. Tadea, newly transplanted to this environment where appearing to be good is more important than actually being good (*T,* 101), is the one to receive punishment. Tadea's situation is very similar to that of Matia in Matute's *Primera memoria (First Memory).* Like Matia, Tadea is exposed to blackmail and false accusations at the hands of her cousins and even the servants because everyone knows that her aunt will presume her to be guilty.

The type of education that Aunt Concha attempts to give Tadea is filled with hopeless contradictions. Tadea is told that she must learn not to cry, but then she is accused of being heartless when she shows no emotion. She is told that it is her obligation as a child to play, but yet her games invariably meet with disapproval. She overhears her aunt say that Tadea herself would have been better off if she had died with her mother, but she is treated as a prisoner when she says, in the heat of anger, that it would have been better if Clota had never been born. Tadea receives no real guidance either from the words or the deeds of her aunt and cousins. Her confusion is further compounded by the actions of Uncle Juan, Concha's liberal and intellectual brother, and Suzanne, who read forbidden books and laugh at some of Concha's rules and regulations. (Suzanne even tends to cross her legs when she sits.) The more Tadea learns of religion, the more her confusion grows. Not only is she told obvious lies — the Virgin Mary also cries whenever children whistle — but she, as a child, is not allowed to ask questions about church teachings or practices. Her nightly prayer, which, like the English equivalent, emphasizes the possibility that she might die before she wakes, creates such fear in the sensitive child that she suffers constant nightmares. The implicit criticism of the inconsistency and ignorance behind the religious upbringing of children in Spain reminds one of the similar criticism in Fernando Arrabal's first novel *Baal Babylone* (1959) and Delibes' more recent *El príncipe destronado* (*The Dethroned Prince,* 1973).

Tadea's anguish is compounded by her separation from her own family. At first, when she came to Santander to be raised with her cousins, she had returned to Galicia in the summer. Later Concha decides that Tadea cannot go home because during the time there she would revert to her old wild ways. The child is not told that there will be no trip to Galicia nor is she allowed to ask, but she can lie awake at night and imagine what it would be like to find herself on the train, homeward bound (*T,* 114–18). The theme of liberty, which will be a dominant one in the second novel of the trilogy, already appears in *Sadness* with reference to Galicia. In Galicia the family dog runs loose, and the children may play with her; in Santander, Diana is always tied up, and little girls are not allowed to play with dogs. In Galicia there are wild horses, horses whose manes are related to Tadea's own long hair. One of Aunt Concha's first acts with Tadea is to cut the child's hair, a gesture which Tina later remarks is also indicative of economic class. In cutting her niece's hair, Concha symbolically cuts off her freedom and indicates that the child will be raised as a servant, not as an equal to Concha's own children. The longer Tadea is away from home, the more she feels abandoned by her father. Although she hears occasional remarks about Gabriel that he is not the kind of man to make trips away from Galicia or to remember to send presents no matter what the event, she tends to give greater credence to Aunt Concha's repeated criticism of a father who does not come for his daughter's first communion or send her presents. Tadea's sense of isolation is clearly expressed in her thoughts when she and Julia walk past an orphanage in the city: "There was no need for bars, she knew that for certain. Bars could be a wall, a garden, an avenue of plane trees, another little girl, the cold voices of grown-ups, the mocking or pitying voices, the laughter of other children, the unctuous voices, sticky like oil. Bars could be what held you back, even when you wanted to, coming from you didn't know where. Maybe in that house the orphans were making fun of me or were looking at me with pity because they knew that a father too can reject his little girl" (*T,* 84). By the end of the novel, Tadea mentally cuts herself off from her Galician past as if she were putting a cover on a well (*T,* 253).

Tadea's reaction to the repressive atmosphere of the house outside Santander is, quite realistically, not an immediate one. Rather the change in her is gradual. Julia, when she comes back a second winter, comments on how quiet Tadea has become. The novel is divided into two parts. In the first, when Tadea has presumably only recently arrived at her grandmother's, she recalls her long conversations with Tina and talks at length to Julia. By the second half, she has become so taciturn that she can express her thoughts to no one. She cannot even show her affection to Julia, although she fights her cousin and soils her first communion dress when Ana makes fun of Julia.

The title of the novel relates directly to Julia, the grandmother's humble and physically deformed cousin. A deeply religious woman, Julia experiences her own sense of inner peace and love; she is not disturbed that she eats with the servants rather than with the family or that she has few worldly possessions. Tadea loves Julia, recognizing in her the fine Christian qualities that Aunt Concha talks about but does not reflect. At one point in the novel Concha refers to Julia's congenital deformity and suggests that normal people should give many thanks to God. Tadea's mental rejoinder is "How many thanks you have to give to God, Julia. And I for you, Julia" (*T*, 112). Julia often talks about a sadness, an emptiness that she feels within her when she is hungry. Ana, Odón, and Clota make fun of this expression, but for Tadea, Julia's favorrite comment has a meaning symbolic of the child's own anguish and loneliness, a loneliness she feels deeply but cannot express at the end of the novel when she receives Julia's prize possession, a chest of drawers, and realizes that this must mean that Julia has died.

Sadness has no real plot; the novel merely relates a child's reaction to the daily events of two years of her life. As Rosario Bofill said in her review, *Sadness* is the relatively rare literary expression of a child's inner world and suffering.[9] In many of her earlier works Quiroga had presented an alienated character whose sense of isolation was the result of a traumatic childhood. With Tadea in this first novel of the trilogy, she gives her most complete development to date of that kind of childhood experience.

II I Write Your Name

To a certain extent, the second novel of the trilogy is a continuation of the first, picking up the day-to-day existence of Tadea at the age of nine, where *Sadness* left off, and carrying her through six years of boarding school to the summer of 1936, just before the outbreak of the Civil War. While *Escribo tu nombre (I Write Your Name)* stands as a separate work, a familiarity with the earlier novel does help orient the reader, particularly in identifying references to certain characters, such as Julia, who appear only in *Sadness.* A careful reading of the two novels does, however, reveal a few minor discrepancies between them. For example, in *Sadness* we are told that Tadea will enter the boarding school in January (*T,* 277); in *I Write Your Name* she actually enters in October.[10] In *Sadness* Tadea's mother had died in childbirth and the male infant had not survived (*T,* 139); in the second novel Tadea's father tells her that her mother died when Tadea was born (*EN,* 388). In *I Write Your Name* Tadea's father also tells her that he has not seen her for four years (*EN,* 387) when, in fact, close analysis of the chronology of *Sadness* would indicate that father and child have been separated for at least five years, for Tadea did not go home to Galicia in the summer of 1930 and it is the spring of 1934 when Gabriel finally comes to visit her at the boarding school. Five years elapsed between the publication of the first novel and the second, thus explaining inadvertent contradiction on the author's part, although the error of Tadea's father in counting the years since he has seen his daughter may be an intentional one, reinforcing Tadea's feeling that her father really does not care about her.

Unlike Quiroga's earlier novels, *I Write Your Name* is quite precise in its chronology. For example, we are told that Tadea enters the school in October, 1930 (*EN,* 77). The seasons of the school year are well defined — Christmas vacation, Easter, summer vacation — and we can therefore date the action at any given point in the novel. In some cases, because of the importance of the political unrest in Spain, Quiroga confirms the historical chronology by referring to specific events. It is from this careful attention to dates in *I Write Your Name* that we can determine the historical time of the action in *Sadness.*

In spite of its status as a sequel to *Sadness, I Write Your Name* differs considerably in structure and style from the first Tadea novel. It is also written in the first person, from Tadea's point of view, but the counterpoint between past and present has disappeared. It is clearly apparent in *I Write Your Name,* as it was not in *Sadness,* that Tadea is recalling the experiences of her childhood and adolescence from the perspective of some unspecified later time. The main body of the novel, pages 77–678, is, as Dámaso Santos has pointed out, almost a traditional novel in that the narrative is handled on only one plane.[11] With the occasional exception of fleeting references to events that have not yet taken place or of digressions in which Tadea gives a general impression of some experience in the school, the narration is linear. Tadea's perspective is sometimes subjective, when she tries to verbalize her own innermost feelings or gives her impression of the sea, but the dominant tone of this portion of the novel is less of interior monologue than of an external reporting of the world around her — the school, her classmates, the nuns, her relatives at vacation time, her grandmother's servants, the rumors of the political conflict in Spain that inevitably filter through the walls of the convent or affect the grandmother's home. It is for this reason that Fernández Almagro has labeled the novel both "social" and "objective."[12]

The pages that precede the main body of the novel are, however, quite different in tone and represent the greatest structural innovation in the work. Following a word to the reader and the Spanish translation of Paul Eluard's poem "Liberty," from which the title of the novel comes, Quiroga presents a sixty-page, untitled section, set in italics and divided into seven short chapters. Like the novel to follow, these pages are written in the first person from Tadea's point of view and deal with her years in the convent school. Unlike the main novel, the section is written in a stream-of-consciousness style without regard for chronology. Tadea, viewing her experience retrospectively, compresses the six years and evokes memories and feelings as they come to mind. Thus she begins her thoughts with the day, when she was thirteen, that she wrote the word "liberty" in her notebook while, in the more detailed, chronological recollection that follows, this event does not occur until page 333. There is no doubt that these first pages contain a subjective, poetic element not emphasized in the main body of the novel. It is as if the character had to purge herself of the emotional reaction to these experiences before she could settle down to a more orderly, dispassionate recounting of the past: "Each word, each event, each person has the weight of what cannot be forgotten, for what bursts forth effortlessly because it conserves the heat with which it was lived."[13] The author herself says that she wrote the poetic synthesis at the beginning of the novel so that she could avoid lyricism in the remainder of the work.[14] Her intention in *I Write Your Name* was to present a "total novel" with both subjective and objective perspectives.[15] José Domingo has called this first section a summary of the plot and ideology of the main novel,[16] but it might be more accurate to consider it an impressionistic memory that precedes the detailed reliving of the past.

The introductory section does not, in fact, outline all major events that take place during the six years in question of Tadea's life, nor does the main novel repeat all of the information presented in the stream-of-consciousness memories. The initial sections of the book do, however, express the philosophical orientation of the novel. The theme of liberty, while not always obvious, underlies all action of the novel in the political background of the Second Republic as well as in Tadea's own life. Quiroga, in her preliminary note to the reader, makes it very clear that her work is aimed at those who, like Tadea, are seeking themselves and the truth, and not at those who merely accept traditional formulas without question.

In the foreground of *I Write Your Name* is Tadea herself, and her adolescent rebellion against society. In this respect the novel is related, as Antonio Vilanova has pointed out, to Carment Laforet's *Nada* (*Nothing,* 1945) and Matute's *First Memory.*[17] On the one hand Tadea's protest is against a particular social institution, namely, the convent school which neither prepares young women for the real world nor treats them as individuals. On the other hand, Tadea's increasing disillusionment with the school and with her family is a normal part of growing up. As a child in *Sadness* she learned that the three kings did not bring gifts to children. In *I Write Your Name* she learns that Uncle Andrés has a mistress and that Uncle Juan has had a series of illicit love affairs and is inclined toward alcoholism. Like Moisés in *The Mask,* Tadea begins to perceive the truth behind the façade of hypocrisy. Even the nuns are not exempt from falsifying reality in order to maintain an illusion. When her classmate Isabel dies following an appendicitis operation, Tadea at first accepts the official story of the little saint who suffered her pain in silence and did not ask for medical help in time (*EN,* 223). Later she learns from the gossip of Elvira that Isabel died because one of the nuns gave the child a laxative rather than call a doctor (*EN,* 409). As is frequently the case in the novels of Matute, Tadea's initiation into the adult world comes through a

series of disillusionments and betrayals.[18] That Tadea's critical view
of the adult world is not unique is emphasized by Uncle Juan, who
advises her in her thirteenth summer to look for the good in people.
He tells her that he was young once, too, and he understands her
feelings (*EN,* 465). Later Tadea decides that the good of Uncle
Juan's liberal political views outweighs the bad of his moral conduct (*EN,* 652).

Tadea's own growth as a person forms only one aspect of the
novel, however, and her questioning of social and religious tradition goes far beyond the normal disillusioning contact of idealistic
youth with the reality of the adult world. Tadea's formative years
transpire against the backdrop of three distinct but interconnected
worlds: the convent school, her grandmother's home, and the
political strife of Spain in the 1930s. The girl's eventual rejection of
the school and her awareness of social injustice represent serious
commentaries on intolerance, hypocrisy, and prejudice.

During Tadea's first three years in the boarding school, she is
generally satisfied to be there. The discipline of the school is rigid
— the girls go from class to class in line by height; they are not
allowed to talk to one another except at certain specified times;
they are under constant surveillance, even while asleep; during out-
door recreation, they are required to speak English — but it is an
improvement over the arbitrary and often severe punishments that
Tadea was subjected to by her Aunt Concha. Tadea finds peace in
the rhythm of the convent life, based on the liturgical year, and in
the possibility of escaping individual attention as one of the group
of eleven boarding students who all dress alike and are expected to
act alike. During the first years at the school she regrets the arrival
of vacation times, although Christmas, when she is alone with her
grandmother, is far more enjoyable than summer when Aunt
Concha, who now lives in Madrid, returns.

With the passage of time Tadea's attitude changes. Some of the
change is due to her reaction to the religious teaching at the school.
A priest's discussion of sin, particularly the sin of looking at one's
own body, disturbs the child: "I felt like crying. Leaning my head
on my arm and starting to cry. I felt indecent, dirty from head to
feet. They were his words that soiled me, they that ruined me: there
was evil where before there was nothing" (*EN,* 216). When she is
given a cilice to wear as self-mortification during Lent, she returns
it to the mother prefect unused (*EN,* 380). When her father comes

to see Tadea, he is allowed only one brief visit. She waits for him anxiously all the next afternoon for a promised outing only to be told afterward that he had not been given permission to return. Tadea is deeply resentful of the convent rules, which made no exception for her individual situation, and of the mother prefect's failure to tell her: "I was no longer a little girl to be deceived in that manner" (*EN,* 394). Tadea senses that her classmates feel as she does about the school: "I feel suffocated by that great clamor of protest around me" (*EN,* 405). She is in sympathy with Carola, an intellectual girl who is in almost constant conflict with the mother prefect and Mother Hornedo because she finds that the individual is not allowed the freedom of her own thoughts.

Tadea's criticism of the convent school is heightened by her increasing sense of social injustice in the outside world. Aunt Concha had always looked down upon people of lower social or economic status than herself and had taught her children to do likewise. The same social prejudice continues in the school. The lay sisters are treated like servants, as is Blanca, the only student on scholarship. The girls at the school are taught charity by having an annual tea for poor children, who are humiliated by the nun who condescendingly tells them of the gratitude they must feel for the clothes and food the wealthy girls have given them (*EN,* 402-4). By the summer of 1934, when she is thirteen, Tadea has learned to dislike the convent: "Nobody ever asked us if we were happy there or if that type of life was damaging to us: I believe that it was precisely a question of damaging us, of breaking our will" (*EN,* 455). Tadea finds it humiliating to have her life programmed for her.

But the fall of 1934 holds a pleasant surprise for the rebellious adolescent girls. Mother Gaytán has been appointed to replace the former mother prefect, and the entire atmosphere of the convent changes. The significance of the change is reflected in the structure of the novel itself, which is divided into two parts: pages 75-486, marking the four years under the first mother prefect and pages 489-678, marking the final two years under the leadership of Mother Gaytán. If Mother Ulía, whom Tadea had learned to dislike intensely, was characterized by her "superior smile," the new mother prefect surprises the girls with her spontaneous laugh. Gradually Mother Gaytán abolishes the rigid rules and the constant surveillance. The girls no longer march to class in line. They are not called to the mother prefect's office for interviews but are free to speak to her whenever they choose to do so. Each girl is treated as an individual who is encouraged to do her best work. Grades are no longer read out weekly in front of everyone, and the good conduct bands, which had previously been awarded with as much attention to the social class of the children as to the merit of the individuals, are also eliminated. When Mother Gaytán discovers that the girls have been required to speak English during recreation — something they do not actually do, faking English instead when they might be overheard — her reaction is typical: "Unbelievable. ... I couldn't speak English while I played" (*EN,* 542).

Mother Gaytán's liberal views on education do not reflect a lesser dedication to religion than that of the previous mother prefect. She is, in fact, a mystic who often lapses into meditation and becomes oblivious to the world around her. She considers her responsibility at the school to be a special gift granted to her by God so that she may transmit His love to the girls (*EN,* 620). If there is any danger to the young women from Mother Gaytán's religious teachings it lies, as the priest who comes during Lent at her invitation says, in their feeling prematurely that they have been called to enter the church. Always willing to listen to the girls and their problems and concerns, from Elvira's boyfriend to Carola's interest in philosophy, Mother Gaytán does not lead the girls to the church by coercion but rather by her own example of total commitment and love.

The world of the school, as previously mentioned, is developed in counterpoint with the world of Tadea's family and the larger social scene. The members of Tadea's own family and the servants are divided in their religious and political views. Aunt Concha's rigid, traditional views are offset by Uncle Juan's liberalism. Tomasa, the cook, whose husband Millán is eventually arrested during worker uprisings in Santander, is in constant conflict with Francisca, the servant who cares for the grandmother in Concha's absence and who, if anything, is even more cruel and uncharitable in her religion than Tadea's aunt. The child, who has always been warned by Aunt Concha and Francisca that she will have to work when she grows up, considers work to be a punishment, and she notes that Tomasa, Millán, and Millán's parents all work very hard indeed while it is not quite clear what Uncle Juan and Uncle Andrés do. In her awakening social conscience, she looks for the explanation why Millán was born in the little house, thus being condemned to poverty and hard work, while she was born in the big house (*EN*, 537). Like her Uncle Juan and the new priest, she is in sympathy with the workers and feels that social change will not come easily but is absolutely necessary.

Quiroga's device for linking the grandmother's house with the Spanish political situation is an obvious one. As Marina Mayoral has pointed out, the intellectual Republican, the traditional middle-class family, the leftist servants, and the rightist servants are all "typical . . . the usual story."[19] She adds that Quiroga gives them individual life by viewing them through the perspective of Tadea. The link between the school and the external political conflict is more subtly developed, however. Some events do, of course, have a direct impact on the nuns; on several occasions they must abandon the school and take refuge in the students' homes because the Republicans have been burning convents. More significant, how-ever, is the parallel between the new freedom and liberalism within the convent and within Spanish society. Mother Gaytán has brought obvious improvements to the school — improvements that benefit the majority of the students. But the parents of the girls fear the effects of this new freedom on their adolescent children. At their insistence, Mother Gaytán is relieved of her post in the spring of 1936 and the repressive system of the past is restored. The girls, in protest, organize a strike, which is quelled when they, in coward-ice perhaps, allow Carola to be expelled as the sole student responsible. For some of the girls, the return to the past is im-possible; ironically, Tadea had thought that in 1936 such things could not happen (*EN*, 641). Elvira pretends that she has a dentist's appointment to leave the school and then does not return. Tadea re-solves that she, too, will not come back in the fall. In microcosm, the situation within the school foreshadows the Civil War in Spain as the right attempts to move the country back to the days preced-ing the Second Republic.

Quiroga reinforces the parallel in at least one other way. Much contemporary literature is off limits for the traditionalists. Aunt Concha feels that García Lorca is immoral (*EN*, 588–89). Carola is severely reprimanded by Mother Ulía for mentioning Ortega (*EN*, 363). Tadea, who has been introduced to Ortega, Unamuno, Valle-Inclán, and various contemporary poets by her Uncle Juan, regrets that in her literature course at school the barrier against the con-temporary writers is absolute (*EN*, 594). Mother Hornedo is so ignorant of major twentieth-century writers that Carola is able to fool her by presenting a well-known poem of Antonio Machado as her own (*EN*, 596-97). Mother Gaytán and the priest she brings to the school are quite different in their knowledge and their attitude, however. The priest is perfectly willing to discuss Ortega's famous statement — I am I and my circumstance — with Tadea, although he disagrees with it. He and Mother Gaytán both, in fact, lean to a kind of Christian existentialism that sounds like pure Unamuno: "It seems to me that in general there prevail in you indifference, routine, lethargy, conformity: I prefer doubt, which is already something positive" (Mother Gaytán; *EN*, 521); "You are going to create yourself.... Man is not himself and his circumstance, as if he were inserted in a landscape; man is his circumstance himself, or the circumstance is God, the other part of man" (the priest; *EN*, 536); "Our life without the resurrection seems absurd" (Mother Gaytán; *EN*, 552). Sobejano has correctly categorized *I Write Your Name* as an existentialist novel for its theme of "the break with the scarcely perceptible imposition of custom and daily routine in order to assume the responsibility of an authentic choice."[20] Quiroga has given political as well as philosophical meaning to the existentialist theme by choosing the thoughts of Unamuno, who was himself so closely tied to the liberal Republican ideals of the pre–Civil War period.

Within the school the personal life of the nuns and their cloister remain matters of mystery and curiosity for the girls. Under Mother Ulía's control, they are not allowed to ask the nuns questions nor are they allowed to see the secret parts of the convent. Mother Gaytán, on the other hand, is perfectly willing to tell them of her years of study and even takes several of the girls to the hermitage where the nuns' cemetery is located. The cloister itself, however, continues to be off limits. At the end of the novel, when Mother Gaytán is gone, Tadea enters the cloister and finds nothing, just bare cells. When she leaves the school, she also feels that she has left nothing behind.

Quiroga has been criticized for this section of the novel, as if her position were an attack on the church. It is a false ending, one reviewer declares: "The nuns have God, they have given Him everything."[21] Quiroga's attack, however, is not on religion or on the church but on the formalist, hypocritical, and sterile tendency that she sees within the church. Throughout the novel she carefully differentiates among the various nuns and priests, some of whom are sympathetic characters and some of whom are not. Vilanova observes that *I Write Your Name* is different from *Nothing* or *First Memory* precisely because of the preoccupation with religion,[22] and the author herself indicates that the novel is directed at those who have personally sought and found God (*EN,* 7): "Fools and children tell the truth. Tadea sometimes tells it, always feels it, goes beyond the mask, lifts it in search of the flesh, the human profile. Including in search of God."[23]

I Write Your Name has been criticized for being too long by some critics,[24] but has also been defended by others. Antonio Viglione feels that we must stand back from the novel to appreciate its marvelous panorama and that the reader must become involved; he praises Quiroga for making us feel the passage of time, the flow of the states of mind, and the psychological development of her characters.[25] Although the primary emphasis is on Tadea, Quiroga admirably differentiates among the girls at the school and also gives us a clear portrait of Tadea's cousins. She consistently shows us how boys and girls are treated differently — Odón has considerably more freedom than Clota but is burdened with the constant knowledge that he must prepare himself for a career — and is particularly sensitive in her treatment of menstruation as a matter of concern to the adolescent girls. Tadea herself, both at home and at school, seeks refuge from the outward attacks of others, notably Aunt Concha and Mother Ulía, by isolating herself from within (*EN,* 253) and taking advantage of the "immense force of silence" (*EN,* 384). Her sense of alienation is increased by her feeling that her father has abandoned her there, a contention that the reader has reason to doubt from his comments of having left her with her grandmother because it was her mother's wish, not his (*EN,* 388).

III   It's All Over Now, Baby Blue

The third novel in the Tadea trilogy, which had not been completed at the time of this writing, continues chronologically from where *I Write Your Name* ends. Having determined that she would not return to the convent school, Tadea decides to go home to her father in Galicia. It is there, far removed from the front lines, that she experiences the Civil War just as the author herself did. Because the setting is that of Tadea's early childhood, the beginning pages

of *Se acabó todo, muchacha triste (It's All Over Now, Baby Blue)*
evoke memories of scenes previously described in *Sadness,* but the
structure here is much more complicated than in the first novel with
an overt juxtaposition of the double consciousness of the young
girl relating her experiences and that of the mature woman who
views the situation from a critical perspective.[26] The latter's commentary is distinguished from the girl's narrative by the use of
italics as well as by stylistic differences.

The title for the novel comes from a song of Bob Dylan and
relates specifically to the Spanish Civil War; the war has brought an
end to many things for Tadea, including the illusions of youth. It is
Quiroga's stated intention in this novel to show the impact of the
conflict on the lives of people in an isolated village untouched by
direct warfare. From her own experience in the war, Quiroga recalls
the dense silence and the noble resignation of those in the village:
"The war and the two bands of brothers reached me through the
interpretation of those silences, through the suggestion of that tre-
mendous resignation, through a climate of grandeur and suffering.
For me it was not a question of reds and blues: it was a question of
Manuel, or of Rogelio, or of Eustagio...."[27] During the years of
the war Tadea develops a group spirit and comes to see that those
on both sides of the conflict are brothers. As she loses her adolescent self-centeredness, the references to the "reds" shift from
"you" to "we." As in *The Mask,* Quiroga also intends to show in
this last novel of the trilogy that in the Civil War there were no
winners, that to be among the victors was meaningless for the
young.

When she began writing *It's All Over Now, Baby Blue,* Quiroga
anticipated that she would complete the work by late 1975.[28] By the
summer of 1976, however, she had discovered that the novel was
demanding far more time from her than she had expected and she
doubted that it would be published before the spring of 1977.[29] Her
experience was, of course, quite consistent with her frequently expressed view that a novel writes itself and dictates its own form to
the novelist.

CHAPTER 6

Profound Present

FOLLOWING the publication of *I Write Your Name* in September, 1965, almost eight years elapsed before Quiroga's next novel, *Presente profundo (Profound Present),* appeared. Considered one of the outstanding novels of 1973 in Spain,[1] *Profound Present* is the shortest of Quiroga's full-length works but structurally among her most complex. In many respects it represents a return to her experimental novels of the 1950s including once again the "superimposed and intersecting planes" that Santos found lacking in the second of the Tadea novels.[2]

Primarily *Profound Present* deals with the lives and deaths of two women who have committed suicide. As the action of the novel begins, Daría, a fifty-nine-year-old baker in rural Galicia, walks out into the sea and drowns herself. This episode triggers the curiosity of Rubén, a young Galician doctor, who evokes memories of Blanca, a wealthy, cosmopolitan young woman who had been his mistress for a time in Madrid and later had died in Holland from an overdose of drugs. As vastly different as the life-styles of these two women were, Rubén, in his "investigation" of their cases, and the reader as well, may conclude that both found themselves in a dead-end situation, suffering from "the horror of nothingness."[3] In contrasting the lives of the two women, neither of whom have anything to live for, it is the author's intention to show that the human condition is basically the same in all social classes.[4]

The novel is not divided into chapters, but, through the use of blank space, it does fall into twenty-one identifiable sections. Fourteen of these are written in the first person from the perspective of Rubén, who indicates to us that he is writing these thoughts. Although a few sections deal with the present and Daría — Rubén relates conversations he hears about Daría and her family and participates personally in the search for her body — most first-person narrative passages are set in the past. In these sections Rubén's thoughts follow no chronological order, and while they emphasize his relationship with, and growing understanding of, Blanca, they also reveal a great deal about his own youth and other friends. The Daría story is largely related in the third person, in chronological order starting with the morning of her suicide and continuing through a period of some days after the discovery of her body and the funeral. In some sections Rubén himself is a participant and is referred to in the third person. The point of view here appears to be that of an unidentified narrator, although James H. Abbott has suggested the possibility that Rubén is writing these passages and has merely introduced himself as a character.[5] Through the use of two points of view, Quiroga manages to develop the subjective narrative of Rubén in the first person in counterpoint with the more objective account of Daría's life.[6]

At the beginning of the novel, Daría's story is presented in alternation with the Rubén-Blanca passages, sections one, three, five, seven, and nine relating the death of the Galician woman. But it is clearly not the intention of Quiroga to develop a counterpoint between two fully distinct plots, as was the structural technique of Faulkner in *The Wild Palms*. From the second section on, Rubén forms a link between the two stories. However, his initial intervention is not in the same time frame as the Daría episodes; although the search for Daría's body is not underway until the fifth section, Rubén already refers quite definitely to her suicide in the second section. The real intersection between the two plots or frames of reference is the fourth section, where Rubén listens to conversation about Daría and her family at the inn where he is staying. The pattern of alternating sections disappears in the second half of the novel, with greater emphasis placed on Rubén and his memories.

Profound Present is most closely related to *Something's Happening in the Street* and *The Sick Woman* among Quiroga's earlier novels, although she has undoubtedly surpassed the achievement of either in the more recent work. Once again, Quiroga introduces a multiperspective technique. Rubén, like the narrator in *The Sick Woman*, hears the testimony of several people connected with Daría, all eager to give their side of the story to the visitor. Thus we have the first-person perspective of Soledad, Daría's friend; Eugenio, her son; Serafín, her husband; and Luisa, her daughter.

In the retrospective sections concerning Blanca, Rubén also evokes the testimony of others: her friends Sabina, Pablo, and Edgar. Although these various perspectives are not presented through interior monologues as in *Something's Happening in the Street,* *Profound Present* is comparable to that novel in its analysis of characters after their deaths. Rubén is a doctor, oriented toward research; as a writer, he approaches the mystery behind the lives and deaths of the two women as an "investigation" (*PP,* 18). In his thoughts, he often directs himself to the dead women, addressing Blanca with the familiar "tú" or "thou" form of "you," and Daría, with the polite form. He wants to examine the case clinically to elucidate the hidden motives: "But my tendency as a student always comes back to me: How did you get to this point? How did it all begin, above all: how did you yourself begin? Take your time, all the time necessary, now only you exist" (*PP,* 87). In essence, Rubén outlines the probing technique that Quiroga has frequently used in uncovering the psychology of her fictional people. *Profound Present* is linked to the earlier novels in other ways as well. The narrator of *The Sick Woman,* while studying the case of Liberata, learned a great deal about herself in the process; Rubén, too, learns about himself simultaneously with acquiring an understanding of Blanca. And Blanca, the superficially carefree, "liberated" woman is the product of a broken marriage, in some respects reminiscent of Agata in *Something's Happening in the Street.* Both Daría and Blanca, like many characters in Quiroga's novels, are actually very private people who cannot communicate their existential anguish to others. Nobody really understands them or even tries to do so until after their deaths. It is symbolic of Daría's life and marriage that her husband Serafín, kneeling in tears next to her body, murmurs to himself, "To do this to me ... to do this to me" (*PP,* 55). Serafín, openly unfaithful to Daría with the young Celia, certainly put himself first in his own thoughts for some time. Blanca, divorced from a first husband and separated from her second husband and her son, has had a series of lovers and an abundance of casual friends, but remains essentially alone. Her situation may well be summarized by the leitmotiv of the song "Strangers in the Night," which appears on three occasions in the novel (*PP,* 26, 51, 162).

Although the book jacket for *Profound Present* suggests that Daría is a simple, direct woman in contrast with the more complex psychology of Blanca, the reasons for Daría's anguish and suicide are not so simple. Certainly, the approach of old age and her husband's infidelity are important factors, but they are only part of the total picture. For Quiroga, as indicated in the title, the past is part of the present: "yesterday is today and everything is today, everything happens now in the present" (*PP*, 11). Thus Daría, in removing her jacket before entering the sea, thinks of her adolescence and Delio. Later, from Soledad, we learn that Daría's father, Isolino, had allowed Delio the use of his fourteen-year-old daughter's body the same way that he might have lent a cart or a cow out for interest (*PP*, 71). The sexually abused girl had been treated as a mere object. Marriage, family, and work, her escape from the humiliation of her youth, had provided only a temporary respite. Now as a wife she had been supplanted by a younger woman. (The similarity between the names Delio and Celia is undoubtedly intentional on the part of the author.) Her children neither need her nor pay any real attention to her. Although Eugenio and his mother made the bakery deliveries together every morning, he had not noticed that Daría had been losing weight until his wife, Amelia, pointed it out to him after her death. And Amelia herself wants to take over Daría's work, thereby treating the older woman again as a mere object to be put in a corner. Daría, who had never established a strong sense of identity as an individual, finds herself dehumanized and empty.

Although Quiroga herself rejects the label "feminist,"[7] the reader may well find a feminist message behind the portrayal of Daría's life. Daría had been exploited as a sex object as a child and had made the mistake of identifying herself with her husband and her children rather than establishing her own identity. Daría's mistake is clearly apparent when one considers the testimony of her friend Soledad, who lives alone and likes it. "Old people get in the way," she tells Rubén, "and I don't say that for myself because, thank God, I don't have anyone to disturb" (*PP*, 72). Later she adds: "It's clear to see that they treated her like a piece of junk, that one isn't even good for that any more, I don't know, look, I'm so happy never to have had any dealings with men, what's mine is mine, and if I'm not good for something I'm not, and if I am good, I am. But no man is going to retire me" (*PP*, 73). Soledad is her own person and therefore is at peace in the solitude that her name suggests.

The explanation for the anguish and ultimate suicide of the wealthy and sophisticated Blanca is not so very different from that of Daría. If Daría suffered as a child from an environment of degeneracy and poverty, Blanca's childhood was no better despite her parents' affluence. Her father, always involved in international business affairs, had no time or interest for her. Her mother, pre-occupied with her own love affairs, treated Blanca as a clinical case, turned over to psychoanalysts from the age of thirteen on. Blanca's first marriage to an older, wealthy man, may have been inspired by the same kind of materialistic concern that led Isolino to leave the door unlocked for Delio. Blanca's second marriage was undermined by the husband's infidelity, as Edgar recalls from the time when he first met the couple in Brazil (*PP,* 137). But the real sense of emptiness in her life stemmed from the loss of her child. Although Edgar recalls that Alex and Blanca treated the little boy like a fancy dog, to be played with at intervals and shown off to friends and then returned to the servants, Pablo, a lawyer, tells Rubén several years after Blanca's death of the efforts he had made to secure for her the right to visit the boy: "Blanca decided at that moment to give everything she had and didn't have to get him back" (*PP,* 159). Like Ventura in *Something's Happening in the Street,* she always carries the child's photograph with her. The tragedy, however, was that the boy rejected his mother. Blanca attempts to escape from reality through visiting nightclubs, drinking, and eventually, drugs. Her path of self-destruction is obviously a more active and dissipated one than Daría's, but the motivation in both cases relates to their alienation from a meaningful family life.

If Soledad and her independence stand in contrast to Daría, Rubén's medical school classmate Marta forms a parallel counterpoint to Blanca. Both young women have an intellectual bent and read a great deal, although their choice of books varies. Rubén recalls that he was introduced to certain French poets — Rimbaud, Apollinaire, Eluard, Prévert — by Blanca and to Hispanic writers and philosophers by Marta (*PP,* 117). Both apparently were initially attracted to Rubén by his timidity and relative immaturity. Both are capable of establishing Platonic friendships with men. Rubén says that in medical school Marta "tried to have us treat her like one of the guys" (*PP,* 95), and Edgar affirms with respect to Blanca that "you could treat her like another man" (*PP,* 137). Superficially, then, both women are educated and emancipated, very different from the traditional image of a young Spanish woman whose whole life revolved around her home. But Blanca is not happy to be free of the traditional woman's role; her active life of parties and nightclubs and her later retreat to the hippie subculture are ways of escaping from the reality of broken marriages and the failure with her son. Rubén recognizes in her a nihilistic desire to destroy herself and whatever surrounded her: "It was nothingness for the sake of nothingness, a systematic negation" (*PP,* 115). Marta, on the other hand, while totally free of family attachments, faces life from a positive point of view and is at peace with herself. When both of her parents were killed in an accident, she pulled herself together and went on with her studies. She is the lover of Rubén's friend, Enrique, but she is not concerned about marriage: "We don't want to place limits on each other, nor turn our deep feeling into an obligation" (*PP,* 149). She also has no great desire to have children for selfish reasons, not for the sake of the child: "I don't have to fulfill myself [by having children], I am already complete" (*PP,* 147). Like Soledad, Marta is a self-sufficient and contented person.

In spite of the relative brevity of *Profound Present,* Quiroga succeeds in evoking the lives of a number of characters, giving contrastive views not only of individual situations but also of parent-child and husband-wife relationships. While in many of her preceding novels, the author tended to present introverted characters who had developed their inability to communicate because of their experience as orphans, in this novel she shows that such generalizations do not hold. Rubén is a timid and withdrawn young man, not because he was raised by people who did not love him but because, as an only child, he was "overprotected to the extreme" (*PP,* 59) by a mother who "lived in a false world, taking refuge" in the child (*PP,* 98). Rubén's mother, in marrying a pharmacist, had lowered her social status, and initially could not face her new reality. By contrast Enrique, also an only child, is not spoiled and suffers none of Rubén's psychological problems; he has always had to help his widowed mother, who supported the child and herself by sewing, apparently not as concerned about her change in social status as was Rubén's mother: "she spoke, but without nostalgia, of the luxury and servants and parties that seemed to have existed in another world" (*PP,* 64). Rubén realizes that children are often a disappointment to their parents and conjectures that his own parents have been brought together by their sorrow over him (*PP,* 91). He has failed them because he chose to become a doctor and perhaps carry on his research in America rather than live with them in Galicia and become a pharmacist. Although Daría and Blanca's stories end in tragedy, *Profound Present* is not a totally pessimistic novel. Rubén has overcome his timidity, and his parents over the years have developed a good marriage. In a physically handicapped youth who works in the pharmacy, they have found a surrogate son who will eventually take over the business.

Quiroga probes in the novel for the truth behind the marriages not only of Daría and Serafín and of Rubén's parents, but also of Daría's son, Eugenio, and Amelia. In his conversations with Eugenio, Rubén quickly discovers that Amelia is suffering a real emotional crisis but that it is useless to attempt to explain this to a primitive man like Eugenio (*PP,* 133). Serafín and Eugenio were both incapable of understanding how or why the former's relationship with Celia could possibly have hurt Daría: "men's affairs are men's affairs ... and have nothing to do with the women" (*PP,* 73). Similarly, Eugenio is incapable of understanding the emotional needs of his wife. Amelia has not been able to have children, and their childless state is a source of anguish to both, but Eugenio, with his "poor understanding of virility" (*PP,* 73) would never consider consulting a doctor to find out if the problem were his, not hers. Following Daría's death, Amelia almost assumes the identity of her mother-in-law. She not only takes over her work, as she has always wanted, but also begins to comb her hair like Daría so that the physical resemblance is striking. The concept of Amelia's existence as a repetition of Daría's is reinforced by a circular aspect in the structure of the novel. In the first section of *Profound Present,* we find a description of Daría baking, working the dough in a round pattern without realizing that she always does so (*PP,* 10). In the final section we have a similar description of Amelia at work, using precisely the same words (*PP,* 167). Rubén suggests that the phenomenon is common, that often when someone dies a particular person or group of people assume the identity of the deceased; he wonders if it is Theo, the hippie songwriter who was with Blanca when she died, who has taken on her role (*PP,* 133).

In some respects *Profound Present* is a synthesis of Quiroga's novelistic work as a whole. As is frequently the case, she carefully describes the locale; here, as in *The Sick Woman* and *The Mask,* the scene shifts from the streets of metropolitan Madrid to the little towns and cities of Galicia. But whether the setting is dominantly rural or urban, whether the characters are highly educated or essentially primitive, she finds that the human drama remains the same. The sophisticated narrator of *The Sick Woman* found her own anguish reflected in the existence of Liberata just as Rubén identifies the parallels between Daría and Blanca. Earlier he had found that through the "cutting glass" of Blanca he had been able to see more clearly the reality of his own environment and his own family (*PP,* 48). Rubén, like Tadea or Moisés from earlier novels, attempts to tear away the outer mask in order to uncover the truth of people's existences, the meaning of life and death. As always, the characters of *Profound Present* find themselves to be solitary individuals. Some of them — Daría, Blanca, or Moisés and Liberata from the earlier novels — respond to their isolation by embarking on a path of self-destruction. But others — Soledad, Marta, and ultimately Rubén — are able to find peace within themselves and are even able to reach out to others.

The relationship between *Profound Present* and Quiroga's earlier works is most important, however, in her treatment of time. The title of the novel itself explains the basic concept behind the author's handling of the flow between past and present in virtually all of her works from *Blood* on; her feeling is not that her characters retreat to the past but that the past lives on in the present. Coindreau, in his introduction to the French translation of *The Mask,* states that in this sense Quiroga's concept of time differs substantially from that of Faulkner: "Because, unlike Faulkner's characters who are prisoners of the past and live immersed in it and cannot rid themselves of it, Moisés sees everything in the present, the past as well as the future."[8] Quiroga quite agrees with this assessment; for her the past does not weigh upon the present but is part of the present.[9] Although this approach to time clearly underlies many of her works, it is in *Profound Present* that she most directly expresses it. The theory is introduced from three different perspectives within the novel. In the opening section, it is the unidentified third-person narrator who comments, with respect to Daría, that "yesterday is today and everything is today" (*PP,* 11). Later Rubén elaborates on the subject as part of a more philosophical analysis. He discusses Hegel's concept of perception, memory, and expectation and then adds his own definition of reality as being only the present, but a present shaped by memory and expectation: "We are within ourselves a trinity of consciousness" (*PP*, 75). For Rubén, time is subjective: "Man and time cannot be disassociated; we form an indissoluble unity, to my way of thinking; 'to be is to be in time,' yes, but even more: in your own time, no other exists, there is not our time but my time, as personal and as untransferable as experience, as religion, as love" (*PP*, 76). It is a thought that Tadea also at least began to express when she decided to leave the boarding school; she did not wish merely to pass time but "to be time itself" (*EN*, 677). The third expression of the "profound present" comes from Marta, in a conversation with Rubén. She repeats the idea that the present moment is everything and that the humanity she loves is the person that "we are right now" (*PP*, 151). She advises Rubén that as he travels and becomes a famous scientist, he will always carry with him aspects of his little town in Galicia and of his childhood home: "Some time you will call it nostalgia, who knows, when you ought to call it dynamic: it is the little death and what lives on, your enlightenment as a man, the torch that you will raise in your hand when you reach the podium" (*PP*, 151).

Although Quiroga does not mention Bergson in *Profound Present,* it is quite clear that her concept of time, as McGloin has already noted, is related to that of the French philosopher.[10] Bergson held that "time is an accumulation, a growth, a duration.... that the past endures, that nothing of it is quite lost."[11] It is in this sense that the death of Moisés' mother is never truly over "because the psychic trajectory followed will endure within consciousness as long as Moisés lives."[12] In Moisés' subjective time, the moment of his tragedy is always part of the living present. Similarly, for Daría the moment of her assault by Delio is still with her when, forty-five years later, she decides to take her own life. Bergson's concept that one goes on "creating one's self endlessly"[13] links his philosophy to existentialism: "For Bergson, as for the later existentialists, becoming is the essence of time."[14] This philosophical concept also underlies much of Quiroga's work, where the treatment of time is closely related to a series of existentialist themes.[15]

Profound Present is the shortest of Quiroga's full-length novels but the most intense of her works. Within fewer than two hundred pages, she not only develops the psychology of three major characters and a number of well-delineated minor ones while creating the differing sociological backgrounds of Madrid and Galicia, but she also presents a work rich in philosophy. It is, as Julio Manegat has said, "a study, almost an anguish, about life, about the meaning of existence, the presence of time, the synchronization of life, and ultimately the reasons for living and dying."[16]

CHAPTER 7

A Multi-faceted Novelist

ON the basis of Quiroga's novelistic production to date, it is difficult to place her within any narrow classification, for she has developed and changed considerably over the years, not only in her narrative techniques but in thematic aspects of her work as well. It is therefore quite true, as Pilar Merrill has noted, that "in her extensive, multifaceted, complex work there is material for numerous studies, analyses and interpretations."[1] She has dominantly been a psychological novelist, probing deep within the inner world of her characters, rather than a social realist, but this has not prevented her from revealing the sociological or geographical background against which her characters function. She has been an innovative novelist, introducing multiple perspectives, simultaneous time, and stream of consciousness to the Spanish novel when these techniques were not yet widely used in her country, but she has also been able to show her skill at other techniques, including objective realism and linear narrative with a constant point of view. Throughout her work there has been a philosophical preoccupation with concepts of freedom, self-identity, faith, and time, but here, as with her narrative techniques, she has constantly evolved. The richness of her work may well be due to her desire to be a "total novelist," one who reflects all tendencies rather than limiting herself to a single objective or subjective perspective on her fictional world.[2]

I Regionalism

When Quiroga first became well known in Spain on the basis of *Northwind,* critics were quick to label her a regionalist because the novel was set in Galicia. Over the years, in part because she has situated some of her works in other locales such as Santander and

116

Madrid and in part because of her structural innovations, critics have ceased to speak of her regionalism. It is nevertheless apparent that Quiroga's ties to Galicia are very strong; the action in seven of her eleven full-length novels and one of her three novelettes takes place completely or predominantly in Galicia.[3] Quiroga herself does not believe that novelistic art can be limited to a region. For her one is simply a novelist, not a Galician novelist or a Castilian novelist or even a Spanish novelist.[4] She points out that Faulkner wrote of Mississippi but that his novels are universal. Nevertheless, she finds that she can only write of what she knows, of what she has lived and felt authentically, and that this applies to "material and human geography." That geography for her includes the city, Madrid, which she has vividly described in *Bus One, The Other City, Something's Happening in the Street,* and parts of *The Sick Woman, The Mask,* and *Profound Present;* Santander, the background for parts of *Sonorous Solitude, Sadness,* and *I Write Your Name;* and, most of all, Galicia.

Although the works in which she deals with Galicia vary considerably in structure and narrative techniques, Quiroga's regionalism manifests itself in similar ways throughout her novels. She makes effective but sparing use of the introduction of characters who speak *gallego.* Always she gives us vivid, often poetic descriptions of the land and the people: the wooded mountains, the sea, the secluded little beaches, the *pazos,* the fishing villages, the bustling port cities. Because she has lived at various times in three of the four Galician provinces, she can present authentic descriptions of the setting and people of the northern and southern as well as the inland and coastal areas of the region. Particularly sensitive is her treatment of the Galician woman. The narrator in *The Sick Woman* notes with dismay how prematurely the fishermen's wives and peasant women age because of their life of hard labor. Similarly the narrator in *The Young Plácida,* in trying to reconstruct the dead woman's life, is saddened by the thought that Plácida always had to work hard, that she never had anything of her own, that she was alone and afraid when her child was to be born. Like so many Galician men, her husband had gone to sea in order to eke out a living for his family. While the narrator cannot put the thought of Plácida's senseless death out of her mind, she finds that Galician women merely accept and forget.

Quiroga's Galician novels are characterized by her frequent use of sensory images related to the region, particularly images of the sea, the wind, and the rain.[5] For Moisés, the alienated protagonist of *The Mask,* one of the few good memories he has is of the smell of the sea. The smell evokes for him a certain nostalgia for Vigo and the house where he lived with his aunt. For the narrator in *The Sick Woman,* her husband's beach property in Galicia is the source both of nostalgia and symbolism, for it represents to her, who has never seen it, some lost part of his youth that he loved deeply. In *Sadness* Tadea thinks of Galicia as symbolic of freedom, for there she had felt loved and had been allowed to roam her father's lands. She remembers the wild horses of Galicia, a symbol obviously related to Tadea herself, whose flowing mane is quickly cut short by her stern and tyrannical aunt.

Although Quiroga has always returned to Galicia as a setting for her fiction, following *Blood* she has tended to treat Galicia only as a partial locale for a given work, typically juxtaposing life in Galicia or memories of the region with experience in the cosmopolitan center or the big city visitor's perspective. In *The Sick Woman* the narrator travels to Galicia from Madrid and returns to the city; although she had lived in Galicia as a child, she is now something of an outsider. The same is true of the narrator in *The Young Plácida* and the doctor Rubén in *Profound Present.* In *The Mask* Moisés' thoughts alternate between scenes in Madrid and memories of childhood and adolescence in Vigo. In *Sadness* Tadea evokes her early memories of Galicia in counterpoint with her later experiences at her grandmother's house in Santander. Through this kind of counterpoint between Galicia and some other setting or perspective, Quiroga succeeds in avoiding the limiting aspects of some regionalistic works. Thus, no matter how faithfully she re-creates the atmosphere of Galicia, she always transcends the regional borders and presents a novel of universal appeal. This is true also because she is primarily a writer of psychological novels, concentrating on the human drama that might have taken place in any similar setting. The decline and fall of the family in *Blood,* for example, might have been the story of any family of the landed gentry in an area where sharp lines were drawn between the social classes. The reaction of the narrator to life in the little Galician fishing village in *The Sick Woman* might well have been the response of any city dweller upon visiting such an isolated place. Quiroga, who tends in her novels to probe within her characters and their pasts to uncover the motivations underlying their deeds, firmly believes that the hidden story of one person can be applicable to the lives of others. With reference to the counterpoint between the lives and deaths of Blanca and Daría in *Profound Present,* the author states: "To be human is to be human, regardless of social class. The two women experience the same feeling about their lives, the same lack of understanding of those who surround them."[6] In her novels Quiroga shows us Galicia as she sees it, with all its unique features, but at the same time she reveals her region to be a microcosm of human existence.

II *Social Commentary*

In the 1950s, when the objective novel of social realism was the dominant current in Spain, Quiroga was concentrating on a more subjective, psychological novel. Paradoxically, however, she not only described the sociological background for her novels but even introduced certain themes of social or political commentary that other writers were not to analyze until the following decade. Reviewing her novelistic production one can find such social awareness in virtually all of her works, to varying degrees.

As with other members of her literary generation, Quiroga is concerned with the Spanish Civil War, the conflict itself as well as its causes and consequences. In *Sadness* and *I Write Your Name* she makes it very clear that the war was inevitable in a nation where such sharp divisions existed between the social classes that even a child like Tadea sensed the injustice of the situation. Tadea's sense of identification with the working class, her critical attitude toward the rigid, discriminatory views of people like her aunt Concha, and her ultimate inability to consider those on the opposite side in the war as her enemies, undoubtedly are feelings that the author herself shares. As early as *Northwind* and *Blood* and throughout the Galician novels in particular Quiroga has shown her sympathy for people from disadvantaged backgrounds who are looked down upon by others in society.

In her treatment of Spanish society Quiroga avoids siding overtly with one social or political group, thereby taking a propagandist stance. She is possibly the first writer in Spain to show consistently that in the Civil War atrocities were committed by both sides, that the brutal slaying of Moisés' parents by the Communists was duplicated by similar crimes of the Nationalists. Her position on the war is that everyone lost and that the aftermath of the war continued for decades to follow. Certainly Moisés continues to suffer its consequences twenty years later, and his niece Felisa firmly believes that all of her parents' generation failed to build a new and better Spain because they could not shake off the animosities of the past. Like Tadea, Felisa is sharply critical of her elders and of the world they have created for the young to inherit. Quiroga does not suggest that these young critics have absolute truth on their side nor does she fail to imply that they are too harsh in their judgment, but undeniably she is sympathetic to their views. It is a repeated tendency in her novels to tear aside the mask of respectability and tradition to reveal the hypocrisy and intolerance of a society that denies equal justice to all or resists social change of any kind.

The Civil War does not become the central theme of a complete novel of Quiroga's until *It's All Over Now, Baby Blue,* but certain aspects of the war and its aftermath were previously apparent in *Sonorous Solitude* and *Something's Happening in the Street* as well as *The Mask.* In the background for her novels, Quiroga includes many other aspects of Spanish society besides the war. In *Something's Happening in the Street* she is among the first Spanish novelists to treat the issue of divorce and the impact it has on all involved, particularly the children, in a Catholic country that refuses to recognize the second marriage as legitimate.[7] Here, as in many of her novels, she writes with great sensitivity of those who are treated as outcasts by society for whatever reason. There is a concern in her works for the institution of marriage and the family, but primarily she stresses the problems of those, like orphans and widows, who are denied the support of close family ties and who therefore find themselves alone.

Quiroga does not consider herself a feminist and does not set out deliberately to depict the status of women in Spanish society, although, to the extent that her works are sociologically accurate such background information is implicit in the novels.[8] Her attitude toward women and their role in life has clearly evolved over the years, however. In her first novel, *Sonorous Solitude,* her main character derives her strength from her husband and desperately wants to have children. In *The Sick Woman* the narrator is troubled that she is childless. By *Profound Present* there are female characters with a strong enough sense of self-identity that they can cheerfully and voluntarily remain single and childless. One of them is a doctor, the first professional woman to appear in Quiroga's novels. With the changing times Quiroga, too, has changed, recognizing that women may achieve self-fulfillment through various lifestyles.

Perhaps the most thorough social commentary in Quiroga's works, however, is in the area of education. In *Sadness* and *I Write Your Name* the author presents a long and detailed indictment of the way children were raised in Spain in the past, clearly criticizing both the training they received in the home and the narrowness of the religious education they were given in the Catholic schools. The censorship of their reading, the social and religious prejudice instilled in them from early childhood on, and the total lack of freedom accorded them are all highlighted in these two novels.

III *Psychological Studies*

Quiroga's primary interest in almost all of her novelistic works, however, has been the inner world of her characters. Most frequently she has displayed a desire to probe deep within the individual to seek explanations for apparently inexplicable acts. Even in *Northwind,* with its omniscient narrator and development of character from without, Quiroga was able to uncover both motivation and human anguish; we come to understand the isolation and hostility of Marcela as well as the reasons why Alvaro married her. By 1953, with the publication of the novelette *The Other City,* Quiroga had begun to use interior monologue and multiple perspectives, techniques quite consistent with her intention of revealing the inner world of her characters. In the following year, with *Something's Happening in the Street,* she continued the use of interior monologue and multiple perspectives while introducing another narrative technique that she was to repeat in several of her most successful psychological studies. Rather than beginning at the beginning and leading up gradually to an event like Alvaro's accident and death in *Northwind* that might appear melodramatic to the reader, she begins after the fact — Ventura is already dead in the opening pages of *Something's Happening in the Street* — and then lets the characters within their own consciousness seek the meaning and motivation behind those events. Why does Liberata lie motionless and speechless in *The Sick Woman?* What is the responsibility of the others for her illness? Why did Moisés of *The Mask* embark upon the path of self-destruction that has led him to his present state of degeneracy? What induced a man of Manuel Mayor's age to return to the bullring in *The Last Bullfight?* Why did Daría and Blanca of *Profound Present* commit suicide?

Sometimes, as in the case of *The Mask* or the first-person narratives in *Sadness* and *I Write Your Name,* the psychological analysis is of the main characters themselves, with only their limited viewpoint on the true nature of the secondary figures. More typically, Quiroga studies several characters simultaneously, while the central figure, because he or she is already dead, is revealed only through the thoughts of others. In *Something's Happening in the Street,* for example, we have Ventura's own thoughts indirectly through the memories of the other characters; the real psychological study here is of those who survive, Ventura's family. In *The Young Plácida* and *The Sick Woman* we have the narrator's analysis of Plácida and Liberata as well as her opinion of other characters based on her conversations with them, but most of all we have the thoughts of the narrator herself as she probes within her own consciousness.

While Quiroga's characters range from primitive peasants to cosmopolitan professional people, she tends in her most thorough psychological studies to delve within the inner world of solitary people who, whatever their social or economic background, find themselves unable to communicate their human anguish to others. Often these introverted figures have been denied a normal family life as children and have withdrawn behind a mask of silence. Even in the cases of Agata in *Something's Happening in the Street* and Blanca in *Profound Present,* apparently happy, carefree young women with active social lives, the truth is that they are hiding their real feelings of rejection. Agata is fortunate in having a sensitive husband who tries to understand her; more typically the characters find themselves completely shut off from others and, like Liberata, Moisés, or Daría, follow varying courses of self-destruction. Perhaps the most representative and the deepest of Quiroga's psychological studies is that of Moisés, orphaned and taciturn like so many of her characters but, in addition, the victim of an incurable guilt complex. In the course of *The Mask* the author carefully shows us how much Moisés needs to confess his crime but how, when unable to do so, he is destroyed by his feelings of guilt and in turn attempts to destroy others.

Although some critics have suggested that Quiroga naturally develops her female characters better than her male characters, and that the latter are weak, this is not really the case. Clearly her most thorough psychological analysis is that of Moisés. Moreover, she has presented convincing portraits of men in the cases of the three bullfighters in *The Last Bullfight,* of Froilán in *Something's Happening in the Street,* and of Rubén in *Profound Present.* However, it is true that she has consistently given us revealing analyses of the female experience: the onset of menstruation *(Sadness, I Write Your Name);* the atmosphere of a girls' school *(I Write Your Name);* the reaction to pregnancy *(Something's Happening in the Street)* or childbirth *(The Young Plácida);* the difficulty of remaining childless in a society that decrees that all women should be mothers *(The Sick Woman, Profound Present);* the trauma of finding oneself cast aside by an unfaithful husband *(Profound Present)* or of finding oneself widowed or divorced *(Something's Happening in the Street).* She develops her female characters with great sensitivity, whether they are young or old, rich or poor, finding a common denominator always in all human experience.

Quiroga's ability to write convincing psychological novels is not mere accident, for she obviously has read extensively in the field. Her knowledge of Freudian theories is particularly apparent in *The Mask,* where young Moisés had become attached to his mother and resentful of his father, and in her careful probing of his childhood to uncover piece by piece the explanation for his present state of mind. In *Profound Present* Quiroga's own study of psychological theory once again surfaces when her characters begin to discuss Fromm and Jung. Moreover, when Daría's daughter-in-law begins to assume certain characteristics of the dead woman, she is manifesting a kind of introjection. In these two novels as well as in *The Sick Woman* Quiroga has presented psychological case studies that might well be analyzed in terms of modern psychiatry.

IV *Structural Innovations*

Of equal importance with the psychological aspect of her novels and closely related thereto is Quiroga's use of innovative structural techniques: interior monologue, stream of consciousness, multiple perspectives, and simultaneous time. All four techniques are associated with Faulkner, and one may well speak of the impact of that

North American novelist on Quiroga even though the Spanish critics in the 1950s who labeled her as a mere imitator of Faulkner were undoubtedly wrong. Like Faulkner himself, Quiroga tends to use a different structure with each major novel. In *Something's Happening in the Street* and *The Last Bullfight* she develops multiple perspectives with a narrative that shifts from the consciousness of one character to another; in form they bear some resemblance to *As I Lay Dying* or *The Sound and the Fury*. In *The Sick Woman* we have the viewpoints of various characters on what might have been the truth of the Liberata-Telmo romance and her peculiar illness, but these viewpoints are presented in testimony to an unnamed narrator, who later analyzes the information in her own first-person interior monologue. Her function as listener might be compared to that of Quentin in *Absalom, Absalom! The Mask*, except for moments of dialogue that Moisés overhears, is written entirely in a stream of consciousness from his perspective, but, like sections of *Something's Happening in the Street, the Last Bullfight,* and *Profound Present,* Moisés is presented through the kind of third-person narrator that Faulkner introduced in *Light in August*. It is, in fact, in this use of a directed third person that Quiroga may be most in debt to Faulkner. *Profound Present,* with its counterpoint between two separate narratives and between the stories of two suicides, Daría's and Blanca's, may be related structurally to *The Wild Palms* or to *Light in August* with its interwoven stories.

Quiroga's tendency to shift from one point of view or narrative level to another initially disconcerted her readers. Such, for example, was the case with *The Sick Woman* where the perspective shifts from that of the anonymous narrator, whose story may well be the principal one of the novel despite the title, to that of the various people in the town who talk to her about Liberata. Quiroga does not wish to give us a simple narrative line that reveals to us the total situation; rather she wants the reader and even the narrator to immerse themselves in the story, to listen to all the testimony, and then to arrive at a conclusion. In her multiperspective novels one can piece the stories together from the various witnesses and then one of the characters — the narrator in *The Sick Woman,* the son-in-law in *Something's Happening in the Street,* Rubén in *Profound Present* — can attempt to synthesize and speculate what must have been, as Quentin and his roommate do in Faulkner's *Absalom,*

Absalom! In these novels as in *The Mask,* Quiroga forces us to participate in the novel, gleaning information bit by bit from the consciousness of the several characters, attempting to reconcile contradictory opinions. Sometimes in the course of the narration she deliberately withholds information. Only near the end of *The Mask* do we know the cause of Moisés' anguish and guilt which always hovered beneath the level of conscious thought throughout the novel. Finally the pieces of the puzzle fall into place. The technique of gradual revelation is present to some extent in Quiroga's novels from *Blood* on but is most fully developed in *The Mask.*

Closely linked with this technique is the fluidity of time so typical of both Faulkner and Quiroga. Quiroga's novels may have an external time of only a few hours — *Something's Happening in the Street, The Mask, The Last Bullfight* — or a few days — *The Sick Woman, Profound Present* — but internal time, which flows from past to present and back again within the consciousness of the characters, may cover a period of many years. Even when Quiroga abandons the shifting levels of narrative and maintains a constant point of view, she generally continues to develop simultaneity of time, as in *Blood, Sadness,* and the opening section of *I Write Your Name.* It is Quiroga's philosophical belief that the past is part of the present, the "profound present" expressed in the title of one novel, and the fluidity of time in her narrative technique responds to this philosophical concept as well as to theories of modern psychiatry.

Although the most obvious structural innovations in Quiroga's novels are ones earlier introduced by Faulkner, in no sense can one limit Quiroga by attributing to her a mere imitation of the North American novelist. Quiroga believes that each novel dictates its own form and, accordingly, in the Tadea trilogy she has returned to a first-person narrative, a point of view that Faulkner himself abandoned. From time to time in her novelistic development she has introduced passages of dialogue that approach objective realism and differ considerably from Faulknerian techniques, as in *Bus One* and parts of *The Last Bullfight.* And in most cases, whatever her narrative technique — objective dialogue, stream of consciousness, etc. — she has been somewhat in advance of the main current of the novel in Spain.

V   Philosophical Implications

Underlying the majority of Quiroga's novels is a religious and philosophical preoccupation little mentioned by critics. *Blood* and *The Other City* at the moment of their appearance led some reviewers to suggest that she was Spain's long-awaited Catholic novelist, but her later criticism of aspects of church teachings and practices in *Something's Happening in the Street, The Mask,* and *I Write Your Name* dispelled that theory. More recently, on the basis of such novels as *I Write Your Name* and *Profound Present,* some writers have begun to see existentialist leanings in Quiroga's philosophy.[9] Quiroga does not consider herself to be a Catholic novelist but she does categorize her work as Christian. In her opinion *I Write Your Name,* with its negative view of Catholic education, is a deeply Christian work. She finds it impossible to discuss the human condition without considering the issue of the individual's relationship with God, and certainly that is one of the issues that concerns Tadea throughout her years in the convent school. Quiroga also agrees with Sobejano that she is an existentialist, although she qualifies the term with the adjective "human." She has always been interested in philosophy and has read extensively in the field. To McGloin several years ago she mentioned the importance of Unamuno for the development of her own thought.[10] At one time she read a great deal of Heidegger, whose philosophical works were readily available in Spain because of his conservative political leanings. In *Profound Present* her personal knowledge of philosophy surfaces when her characters discuss Hegel.

From *Blood* on Quiroga has shown a basic preoccupation with the meaning of life and death. In this respect her characters often reflect an appreciation of the "tragic sense of life" associated with Unamuno's philosophy. The chestnut tree in *Blood,* witnessing the passions and struggles of the human inhabitants of the nearby house, frequently notes that their love-hate conflicts are stilled by the passage of time and the inevitability of death, yet the people live on to some extent in their descendants who represent a kind of immortality. The doctor in *The Other City* also discovers death and its mystery; in spite of his science, he cannot save the lives of terminally ill children. In these early works Quiroga appeared to resolve the anguish that the knowledge of death creates by seeking the consolation of the church. *Blood* is filled with religious symbolism, particularly references to the cross, and the doctor in *The Other City* decides to become a priest. Gradually, however, Quiroga begins to question the institution of the church itself. The priest in *Something's Happening in the Street,* reminiscent of Unamuno's San Manuel, is willing to conjecture that Ventura, had he been able to speak, would have confessed his sins, sought reconciliation with the church, and died in a state of grace. He is, of course, bending church doctrine to establish forgiveness for a man who had, in the eyes of the church, lived in sin because of his divorce and second marriage. In *The Mask* Quiroga continues her use of religious symbolism but shows quite clearly that the representatives of the church were unwilling or unable to offer Moisés the help he sought through the confessional. At the time of *I Write Your Name,* the novelist expresses overtly in her introductory passage the belief that each individual must seek God on his or her own. Her position is still profoundly Christian, but she has rejected the institution of the Catholic church as an intermediary between the individual and God.

Throughout her novelistic development Quiroga has articulated themes of freedom and solitude, concepts that relate both to her growing disillusionment with institutionalized religion and to her increasing emphasis on existential philosophy. Her characters are often solitary, even alienated individuals who know that they must seek the meaning of their lives within themselves; like Tadea they insist upon the liberty to do so. Such a viewpoint is closely related to that of existentialism: "The self that existentialism seeks is each person's individual self, which he must forge for himself out of such senseless circumstances, such meaningless limitations, as are given to him."[11] The individual has the freedom to shape his or her own identity, but with that freedom goes responsibility. Quiroga goes beyond merely symbolizing freedom through such images as the sea *(Blood),* bulls*(The Last Bullfight),* and wild horses *(Sadness)* to insist upon responsibility in a Sartrean sense. Felisa in *The Mask* accuses the older generation of using the "senseless circumstances" of the Civil War as an excuse for failing to take positive action. For her even Moisés is to blame for his own destiny. The progressive priest in *I Write Your Name* thus rejects Ortega's formula "I am I and my circumstance" because the individual should transcend and indeed mold that circumstance as part of himself. Among Quiroga's characters there are at least two who behave as existentialist heroines, willing not only to accept their freedom and act but also to assume full responsibility for those acts. Presencia in *Something's Happening in the Street* has been faithful to her own conscience and is able to withstand society's ostracism for the choices that she has made. Carola in *I Write Your Name* expresses what she believes and with dignity accepts her punishment — expulsion from the convent school — assuming responsibility for the group even though her classmates are too cowardly to stand with her.

In some of Quiroga's works certain characters experience moments that could be categorized as existential awakenings: "Existentialism emerges as a philosophy which demands a radical, personal, and never-ceasing questioning of the purpose of human life."[12] When the narrator of *The Sick Woman* confronts the reality of Liberata, she suddenly becomes aware of the absurdity of life. When Rubén of *Profound Present* learns of Daría's suicide he, too, must begin to question the meaning of existence. In both cases it is the awareness of another person that leads the character to meditate not only on life itself but on his or her personal existence and its meaning. Their reaction is not unlike that of the Christian existentialist Gabriel Marcel: "It is in so far as I believe in the existence of others and act on that belief that I affirm my own existence; similarly, it is genuine response to another that initiates and can sustain the creation of my own being in fidelity."[13] This is certainly the basis of the existential awakening of Anuncia in *Bus One* who suddenly is conscious of the existence of herself and others. In *The Sick Woman, The Young Plácida,* and *Profound Present* the narrators and Rubén seek themselves and the whole human tragedy through the revealing mirror of the other life with which they have come in contact.

It is important to these characters that the self they identify be an authentic one. They share with existentialist thought in general "the hostility to closed systems, secular or religious, which pretend to be exact mirrors of what the world is all about,"[14] because such systems may deny to the individual the right to develop an authentic self. The rejection of all inauthenticity is particularly apparent in the character of Tadea in *I Write Your Name* but is also the basis of Rubén's self-questioning or even of Ventura's divorce. In contrast to the characters in Quiroga's novels who are seeking themselves are others, like Ventura's first wife and some of Moisés' cousins, who hide behind a mask of hypocrisy and deny their own identity, even to themselves. The most anguished of her characters, however, are those like Moisés and Blanca who can neither find themselves nor yet be content with an inauthentic identity; these characters eventually destroy themselves or others. Some few of her characters, either through religion or philosophy, are able to find peace with themselves and accept themselves for what they are. This group is a varied one, ranging from the humble Julia of *Sadness,* who finds her strength in her faith, to the intellectual Marta of *Profound Present.*

Consistent with Quiroga's existentialist thought is her treatment of time. Just as *Profound Present* is the culminating expression of her philosophy, so it is the most overt expression of her concept of time. The present is deep because it includes both past and future. Time is subjective, existing only as perceived by the individual. Quiroga follows Bergson in her acceptance of the concepts of duration and simultaneity: "Duration is essentially a continuation of what is no longer in what is."[15] "Simultaneity would be precisely the possibility for two or more events to enter a unique and instantaneous perception."[16] The characters in *Profound Present* openly discuss this concept of time, which is also essentially existential time,[17] but they and other characters in Quiroga's earlier works have also lived it. When Daría is about to throw herself into the sea, she finds thoughts of her adolescence present in her consciousness. Tadea in *Sadness* experiences at one and the same time her childhood in Galicia and in Santander. The use of simultaneous time is present in other works, including *Something's Happening in the Street, The Sick Woman,* and *The Last Bullfight,* but reaches its highest level of development in *The Mask.* It is quite clear that the past continues to live for Moisés; his present includes all of his past experience. Quiroga notes that her concept of time may well have evolved because of her readings in existentialist philosophy but that in *Profound Present,* she is also influenced by Fromm and Jung. Psychiatry, particularly existentialist psychiatry, overlaps philosophy and shares certain views on time and self-identity: "Man's most human faculty is his awareness of his identity of himself as a distinct person who exists in a continuum of past, present, and future and who plans and shapes his own fate with a sense of self-determination."[18] This is a concept that underlies much of Quiroga's work from 1953 on. In *Blood,* which antedates that period, she depicted characters not totally free to develop themselves because of heredity and, despite a certain fluidity of time in the narration, she dominantly portrayed a concept of natural or eternal time. In these respects *Blood* stands apart from all her later novels.

When one takes Quiroga's work in its totality, a pattern emerges with respect to the philosophical implications of her fiction. In any given work, however, she does not present a rigid position as to what one should believe or be. She tends to treat all of her characters sympathetically no matter what their religious or philosophical stance. Among her admirable characters one may include the mystical nun in *I Write Your Name* and the atheistic second wife in *Something's Happening in the Street.* Quiroga views with the same human compassion the alienated Moisés, who is both victim and assassin; the primitive Plácida who accepted her humble life without question; the young Tadea, who is seeking her authentic self; and the introspective Rubén, who probes within his own life and that of others in search of the meaning of life and death. The author's goal is to create not an existential novel but a total one, one that will reflect all tendencies.[19] Accordingly, she does not wish to espouse a particular outlook on life but rather prefers to present a fictional world inhabited by a diversified group of people representing different social classes, different educational levels, different religious beliefs. Ultimately what interests her is the inner drama of the individual and its relationship to the human condition. By probing deep within the consciousness of her characters she hopes to show us something of the meaning of existence for us all.

Notes and References

Chapter One

1. Unless otherwise indicated, opinions and statements attributed to Elena Quiroga are drawn from taped interviews that the present writer made with the novelist on June 9 and June 27, 1975. Here, as elsewhere in the book, all translations are my own.

2. Pedro Rodríguez, "Elena Quiroga veinte años después," *El Siglo* (Bogotá), May 30, 1971, p. 2.

3. A. García Pintado, "Elena Quiroga o la pasión de vivir," *ABC,* March 1, 1967, unpaged.

4. Maurice E. Coindreau, prologue *La careta* by Elena Quiroga (Madrid: Ediciones del Centro, 1974), p. 9. This appeared originally as the prologue to the French edition of *La careta* (1959).

5. García Pintado.

6. Eugenio G. de Nora, *La novela española contemporánea (1927–1960)* (Madrid: Gredos, 1962), vol. II, pt. 2, p. 66.

7. For example, J. M. Martínez Cachero (*La novela española entre 1939 y 1969; Historia de una aventura* [Madrid: Castalia, 1973], pp. 151–53) identifies the period 1951–1962 as being one of the "objective narrative" and of "social realism."

8. *La novela española actual (Ensayo de ordenación)* (Madrid: Editorial Cuadernos para el Diálogo, 1971), pp. 158–75.

9. *Cuadernos de la Romana* (Barcelona: Destino, 1975), p. 247.

10. Rodrigo Rubio, *Narrativa española, 1940–1970* (Madrid: E.P.E.S.A., 1970), p. 76.

11. García Pintado (see note 3) erroneously states that Quiroga has a son. Apparently he believed that the nephew was her child. While helpful in many respects, this particular interview contains a number of errors.

12. Ibid.

13. Janet Winecoff Díaz, who has done extensive research on the contemporary Spanish novel, recalls that Quiroga mentioned a possible five-novel cycle in an interview with her (letter to the present writer, July 24, 1975).

14. Julio Trenas, "Así trabaja: Elena Quiroga," *Pueblo,* April 25, 1957, p. 16; and Mercedes F. Gordon, "Ser novelista es más que una profesión," *Ya,* April 9, 1967, unpaged.

15. The Spanish day, of course, is quite different from the North American one. Spaniards tend to eat their big meal of the day between one and four o'clock. Supper, which is generally a light meal, is not served until 10 P.M. Quiroga thus does her proofreading after lunch, sets aside time from six to seven o'clock to rest, leaving the presupper hours open for relaxation with family and friends.

16. Perhaps the only critic to reject this widespread theory was Joaquín de Entrambasaguas. (See *Las mejores novelas contemporáneas, volume 12 (1950–54)* [Barcelona: Planeta, 1971], p. 1287.) It is probably because of this early labeling of Quiroga's works as naturalistic that she is often erroneously classified as a writer of social realism.

17. Federico Carlos Sainz de Robles, *El espíritu y la letra (Cien años de literatura española: 1860–1960)* (Madrid: Aguilar, 1966), p. 221.

18. Entrambasaguas, p. 1284.

19. Benito Varela Jacome was still presenting the Quiroga-Pardo-Bazán relationship as fact as late as 1963. (See "Viento del norte," *Destino,* March 2, 1963, p. 3.)

20. Coindreau, p. 12. In his opinion on Faulkner's use of time, Coindreau is consistent with the judgment of Sartre, but later critical analysis has established that only some of Faulkner's characters are "prisoners of the past" and that Faulkner's general treatment of time is, in fact, almost identical to Quiroga's. See George C. Bedell. *Kierkegaard and Faulkner: Modalities of Existence* (Baton Rouge: Louisiana State University Press, 1972).

21. The critics have generally failed to note the possible influence of Faulkner on *Blood.* In our taped interview of June 12, 1976, Quiroga indicated that the only novel of Faulkner that she had personally read when she began writing herself was *Sanctuary,* but she was willing to admit the possibility of a certain indirect influence of Faulkner on her work.

22. Quiroga's feeling that Valle-Inclán had influenced Faulkner was reinforced by her conversations with Coindreau who told her that Faulkner acknowledged a firsthand acquaintance with Cervantes and other Hispanic writers. Having personally noted a curious parallel between a scene in Valle-Inclán's *El ruedo ibérico,* where it becomes impossible to transport a corpse to a nearby town for burial because of a flash flood, with a similar scene in Faulkner's later novel *As I Lay Dying,* I was very interested to learn that Quiroga has also identified this particular scene as one in which Valle-Inclán might have influenced Faulkner. The possibility that Faulkner personally knew Valle-Inclán's works opens up a fascinating potential area of research, but my own investigations up to the present have uncovered no evidence to support the theory. A further discussion of Faulkner's possible influence on Quiroga appears in Chapter 7. See also my forthcoming article "Faulkner in Spain: The Case of Elena Quiroga," *Comparative Literature Studies.*

23. Trenas.
24. Ibid.
25. García Pintado.
26. Ibid.
27. Gordon.
28. Rodríguez.
29. Josep Sotes, "Elena Quiroga, *Presente Profundo*," *Diario de Mallorca*, Aug. 22, 1973, p. 30.
30. Rodríguez.
31. Rafael Uribarri, "Elena Quiroga habla para *Diario de Navarra*," *Diario de Navarra*, June 22, 1969, p. 27.
32. Gordon.
33. Rodríguez.
34. José Julio Perlado, "Elena Quiroga, candidata española al premio Rómulo Gallegos," *El Alcazar*, March 31, 1967, p. 12.
35. Miguel Fernández-Braso, "Elena Quiroga. Al margen de la confusión," *Pueblo*, May 12, 1971, p. 4.

Chapter Two

1. Taped interview, June 9, 1975. References to *Sonorous Solitude* are to the original edition (Madrid: Espasa-Calpe, 1949) and are cited in the text as *S*.
2. "La soledad sonora," *Cuadernos de Literatura* 6 (1949), 295.
3. "The Novels of Elena Quiroga," *Hispania* 42 (1959), 210.
4. Angel Valbuena Prat. *Historia de la literatura española*. 7th ed. (Barcelona: Gustavo Gili, 1964), III, 857.
5. Lucile K. Delano ("The Novelistic Style of Elena Quiroga," *Kentucky Foreign Language Quarterly* 9 [1962], 61–67) has pointed out the solitary nature of many of Quiroga's characters, although she fails to note how many of them are orphans.
6. Antonio de Hoyos, *Ocho escritores actuales* (Murcia: Aula de Cultura, 1954), p. 111.
7. De Nora, p. 164.
8. See Janet Winecoff Díaz, *Miguel Delibes* (New York: Twayne, 1971).
9. See, for example, Corrales Egea, p. 125; Entrambasaguas, *La mejores novelas contemporáneas*, p. 1291; Obdulia Guerrero, "Miguel Delibes y su novela 'Cinco horas con Mario,' " *Cuadernos Hispanoamericanos* 210 (1967), 619–20.
10. Juan Luis Alborg, *Hora actual de la novela española* (Madrid: Taurus, 1958), pp. 191–93.
11. Egea, p. 116.
12. De Nora, p. 166.

13. *Las mejores novelas contemporáneas,* p. 1287.
14. Brent, p. 210.
15. E. Correa Calderón, "Galicia a través de *Viento del Norte,* de Elena Quiroga," *Correo Literario,* May 15, 1952, p. 5.
16. Taped interview, June 9, 1975.
17. My judgment here coincides with that of Correa Calderón.
18. Delano, p. 65.
19. Hoyos, p. 98.
20. De Nora, p. 166.
21. *Viento del norte,* 7th ed. (Barcelona: Destino, 1965), p. 17. References are to this edition and are cited in the text as *N.*
22. See Lucile K. Delano, "Sensory Images in the Galician Novels of Elena Quiroga," *Kentucky Foreign Language Quarterly* 10 (1963), 59–68.
23. Alborg, pp. 194–95.
24. De Nora, pp. 166–67.
25. Manuel de Montoliu, "Sangre y alma," *Diario de Barcelona,* May 3, 1953, p. 18.
26. Ibid.
27. Hoyos, p. 106.
28. Prologue *La condesa de Pardo Bazán y sus linajes (Nobiliario)* by D. Válgoma y Díaz-Varela (Burgos, 1952), pp. 7–14. The references that follow are all to p. 8.
29. *La sangre,* 4th ed. (Barcelona: Destino, 1971), p. 189. References are to this edition and are cited in the text as *B.*
30. Quiroga mentioned this particular novel of Faulkner to the present writer during our taped interviews of June, 1975, although she did not specifically suggest a link between *Absalom, Absalom!* and *Blood.* In our subsequent interview of June 12, 1976, she clarified that she had not personally read that particular novel of Faulkner until 1958.
31. Taped interview, June 27, 1975.
32. Delano makes this observation in "The Novelistic Style of Elena Quiroga," pp. 64–65.
33. See de Nora, p. 167, and Gonzalo Sobejano, *Novela española de nuestro tiempo (en busca del pueblo perdido)* (Madrid: Prensa Española, 1970), p. 183.

Chapter Three

1. Benito Varela Jacome, "Cambio del enfoque narrativo de Elena Quiroga," *Destino,* January 26, 1963, p. 36.
2. José Francisco Cirre, "El protagonista múltiple y su papel en la reciente novela española," *Papeles de Son Armadans* 33 (May, 1964), 159. Cela's *La colmena* was originally published in Argentina where Romero was residing at the time he wrote *La noria.*

3. *La novela social española (1942–1968)* (Barcelona: Seix Barral, 1968), p. xvi.

4. M. Fernández Almagro, "*Plácida, la joven,* por Elena Quiroga," *ABC,* August 4, 1957, unpaged; Entrambasaguas, p. 1303.

5. Almagro.

6. José María Javierre, "Notas a 'La sangre,' de Elena Quiroga," *Incunable* (Salamanca), February, 1953, p. 11. Fernández Almagro may have had a similar thought in mind when he compared this novel to works of the French Catholic novelist François Mauriac. See "*La sangre,* por Elena Quiroga," *ABC, January 25, 1953, p. 41.*

7. Quiroga's husband observed in an interview that *Blood* was an essentially Spanish novel because of its emphasis on the idea of God, its preoccupation with death, and its pathos. See Rafael Vázquez-Zamora, "Elena Quiroga, al publicarse *La sangre,*" *Destino,* January 3, 1953, p. 19.

8. *Plácida, la joven y otras narraciones,* 2nd ed. (Barcelona-Madrid: Noguer, 1970) p. 192. References to the short novels are to this edition and are cited in the text as *P.*

9. De Nora, p. 171.

Chapter Four

1. See, for example, Alborg, p. 196; de Nora, p. 167; Domingo Pérez Minik, *Novelistas españoles de los siglos XIX y XX* (Madrid: Guadarrama, 1957), p. 339; Juan Ignacio Ferreras, *Tendencias de la novela española actual 1931–1969* (Paris: Ediciones Hispanoamericanas, 1970), p. 148. At least some of the critics who have labeled *Something's Happening in the Street* as Quiroga's first innovative work apparently are unfamiliar with the two short novels that preceded it.

2. Taped interview, June 9, 1975.

3. In a taped interview with the present writer on June 27, 1975, Quiroga indicated that the subject of divorce began to interest her after a relative's husband abandoned his family and the child felt guilty that she had done something to cause the tragedy. Moreover, Quiroga felt that others ostracized the child, punishing her for a situation over which she had no control. Quiroga herself believes that divorce is bad when it hurts the children, but that divorce should be permitted as preferable to the hypocrisy of a bad marriage.

4. *Algo pasa en la calle,* 3rd ed. (Barcelona: Destino, 1968), p. 161. References are to this edition and are cited in the text as *SH.*

5. Fernando Baeza, "Elena Quiroga *Algo pasa en la calle y La enferma,*" *Indice* 84 (September, 1955), 23; J. L. Vázquez Dodero, "Novela y psicología," *Nuestro Tiempo* 9 (1955), 120; M. Fernández Almagro, " 'Algo pasa en la calle' por Elena Quiroga," *ABC,* January 9, 1955, p. 35.

6. De Nora, p. 168; Ferreras, p. 148.
7. Vázquez Dodero, p. 121.
8. See Chapter 2, note 9.
9. Díaz, p. 142.
10. Entrambasaguas, " 'Algo pasa en la calle' por Elena Quiroga," *Revista de Literatura* 6 (1954), 85.
11. Díaz. p. 142.
12. Sobejano, p. 184. In our interview of June 12, 1976, Quiroga indicated that she did not read *As I Lay Dying* until after she wrote her own novel.
13. See Francisco Ynduráin, "La novela desde la segunda persona: análisis estructural," in *Clásicos modernos: Estudios de crítica literaria* (Madrid: Gredos, 1969), pp. 215–39.
14. Taped interview with Quiroga, June 27, 1975.
15. Baeza.
16. Julio Sigüenza, "Elena Quiroga: 'La enferma' (Novela)," *Faro de Vigo,* August 26, 1955.
17. Baeza.
18. See Laurent LeSage, *The French New Novel* (University Park, Penn.: Pennsylvania State University Press, 1962).
19. Sobejano, p. 184.
20. J. M. Castellet, "La enferma," *Revista,* June 23, 1955.
21. J. V., "'La enferma,' de Elena Quiroga," *La Voz de Galicia* (La Coruña), June 17, 1955.
22. Entrambasaguas, "Quiroga, Elena: *La enferma,*" *Revista de Literatura* 7 (1955), 254.
23. "Tres novelistas españolas," *Revista Hispánica Moderna* 31 (1965), 424.
24. "The Novelistic Style of Elena Quiroga," p. 64.
25. *La enferma,* 2nd ed. (Barcelona, Noguer, 1962), p. 112. References are to this edition and are cited in the text as *E.*
26. Sobejano, p. 184.
27. "'La enferma' por Elena Quiroga," *ABC,* August 14, 1955, p. 59.
28. See P. Z. Boring, "Feminine Roles and Attitudes Toward Marriage in the Comedies of Miguel Mihura," *Romance Notes* 14 (1973), 446–47.
29. Sigüenza.
30. J. L. Cano, "Quiroga, Elena: *La careta,*" *Nuestro Tiempo* 20 (1965), 115.
31. Alborg, p. 197.
32. See E. W[arletta], La generación del desánime," *Cuadernos Hispanoamericanos* 37 (1956), 104–5; Brent, p. 212; Sobejano, p. 186. The latter critic has, in fact, suggested that Moisés' father might just as easily have been attacked by thieves, thus failing to see any of the psychological implications of the father's being in hiding or of Moisés' feeling of

guilt with respect to his mother. The child's response at the time of the killings to some extent reflects the climate created by the tensions of the war.

33. Sister Genevieve Gabrielle McGloin, *Elena Quiroga's "La careta":
Time and the Mask* (Ph.D. diss., St. Louis University, 1971), p. 74.
McGloin's thesis contains a very thorough and perceptive analysis of some aspects of Quiroga's novel: the stream-of-consciousness style, the relationship to existentialism, the alientated hero. Unfortunately, it is marred by some errors in interpretation, the most important being McGloin's contention that it is Moisés who betrays his father, telling the enemy directly or indirectly where his father is hiding. In her taped interview with the present writer on June 9, 1975, Quiroga rejected this theory, indicating that no such secret guilt underlies Moisés' thoughts. The author explains that some neighbor undoubtedly heard the father's movements in the apartment or saw him through the window from an adjoining building and informed the leftist soldiers.

34. *La careta,* 2nd ed. (Barcelona: Noguer, 1963), p. 44. References are to this edition and are cited in the text as *C*.

35. McGloin, pp. 120–21.

36. *Cuadernos Hispanoamericanos* 75 (1968), 638–48.

37. McGloin, pp. 115–17.

38. Cano wonders if Quiroga's primary purpose in writing *The Mask* is to discuss a sexual deviant; if so, he feels that the theme is an inappropriate one. Quiroga was frequently criticized in the 1950s for introducing sexual elements which today do not, of course, seem shocking at all.

39. See, for example, Corrales Egea. pp. 158–75; and Sobejano, p. 44.

40. Coindreau, p. 11.

41. Taped interview, June 27, 1975.

42. McGloin, pp. 159–61.

43. Taped interview, June 9, 1975. McGloin attributes the idea that *The Mask* is a *roman à clef* to Benito Varela Jacome, with whom she had discussed the novel.

44. *La última corrida* (Barcelona: Noguer, 1958), p. 226. References are to this edition and are cited in the text as *U*.

45. Yayo Huertas, "Elena Quiroga y *La última corrida,*" *El Ruedo,* April 11, 1967, unpaged.

46. A. F., "La última corrida," *Indice,* August, 1958, p. 24. Fernández Almagro makes almost the same observation in his review appearing in *ABC,* May 18, 1958.

47. Corrales Egea suggests making the comparison between the two novels (p. 119). There are a number of noteworthy differences, however. De Lera's novel is written in a much more traditional style and leads inevitably to the death of the young bullfighter in his first bullfight. It is intended to be a criticism of the exploitation of the bullfighting world, while Quiroga makes no apparent judgment on bullfighting.

48. A full program in an afternoon would include six bulls.

49. "La última corrida," *El Libro Español* 2 (1959), 318.

50. De Nora, p. 170; and Corrales Egea, p. 119.

51. De Nora, p. 170.

52. Male critics frequently criticize women writers for writing about women rather than men, although one might observe that male writers generally also tend to emphasize their own sex. In the contemporary Spanish novel Elena Quiroga and Ana María Matute, both of whom have written of male characters to a large extent, usually escape from this kind of negative observation.

53. Egea, p. 119.

54. "Nueva novela de Elena Quiroga," *La Vanguardia Española,* May 27, 1958.

55. A. F.

Chapter Five

1. Letter from the novelist, November 5, 1975.

2. McGloin, p. 62.

3. As previously mentioned, *Sadness* won the Premio de la Crítica in 1960 and *I Write Your Name* was chosen to represent Spain in the International Rómulo Gallegos novel contest. Rubio points out (p. 77) that *Sadness* won its literary prize despite negative criticism from Alborg in *La Estafeta Literaria.*

4. McGloin, p. 62.

5. Letter from the novelist, November 5, 1975.

6. Le Sage, p. 5.

7. *Primera memoria* is the first novel in a trilogy which Matute calls *Los mercaderes (The Merchants);* the American translation is called *School of the Sun.* Because of the relationship between Tadea and Quiroga's own experience, it is quite obvious that the situations and characters in *Sadness* are not influenced by Matute's novel. Nevertheless, there are a number of interesting aspects in common. Matia too is motherless, has memories of the servant who raised her, has been abandoned by her father, is victimized by a hypocritical cousin, and finds the atmosphere of her maternal grandmother's house to be repressive.

8. *Tristura,* 2nd ed. (Barcelona and Madrid: Noguer, 1965). References are to this edition and are cited in the text as *T.*

9. "Una infancia sin ternura," *El Ciervo* 92 (1961), 12.

10. *Escribo tu nombre* (Barcelona-Madrid, Noguer, 1965), p. 77. References are to this edition and are cited in the text as *EN.*

11. "Elena Quiroga, *Escribo tu nombre,*" *Pueblo,* November 12, 1965.

12. "*Escribo tu nombre* de Elena Quiroga," *ABC,* November 4, 1965, "Mirador Literario," p. 2.

13. Marina Mayoral, "Una lucha nunca acabada," *Cuadernos Hispanoamericanos* 69 (1967), 553.

14. Taped interview, June 27, 1975.

15. Letter from the novelist, November 5, 1975.

16. "Dos novelistas españoles: Elena Quiroga y Daniel Sueiro," *Insula* 232 (1966), 3.

17. "*Escribo tu nombre* de Elena Quiroga," *Destino,* December 18, 1965, p. 73.

18. For a discussion of this theme in Matute's works, see Margaret E. W. Jones, *The Literary World of Ana María Matute* (Lexington: University of Kentucky Press, 1970).

19. Mayoral, p. 554.

20. Sobejano, p. 188.

21. Esteban Molist Pol, "La adolescencia en una obra de Elena Quiroga," *Diario de Barcelona,* October 30, 1965, p. 12.

22. Vilanova.

23. Letter from the novelist, November 5, 1975.

24. Domingo.

25. "Elena Quiroga *Escribo tu nombre,*" *La Voz de España,* November 12, 1965.

26. All information about *It's All Over Now, Baby Blue* is based on taped interviews with Quiroga on June 9 and 27, 1975. At that time she read me the opening pages of the novel while outlining her intended purpose.

27. Pilar Equiza, "Elena Quiroga y la novela española de posguerra," *Mundo Hispánico,* March, 1976, p. 10.

28. See my note in *Hispania* 59 (1976), 154–55.

29. Taped interview June 12, 1976.

Chapter Six

1. James H. Abbott, "Elena Quiroga, *Presente profundo,*" *Books Abroad* 48 (1974), 544.

2. Santos.

3. *Presente profundo* (Barcelona: Destino, 1973), p. 16. References are to this edition and are cited in the text as *PP.*

4. Taped interview, June 27, 1975.

5. Abbott, p. 543.

6. Miguel Fernández-Braso, "La tensa narrativa de *Presente profundo*" *Pueblo,* June 28, 1973, p. 4.

7. Taped interview, June 27, 1975.

8. Coindreau, p. 12. See Chapter 1, note 20.

9. Taped interview, June 9, 1975.

10. See McGloin, "Chapter One; Time Immeasurable."

11. Will Durant. *The Story of Philosophy* (New York: Simon and Shuster, 1953), p. 338.

12. McGloin, p. 14.

13. Durant, p. 338.

14. Margaret Church. *Time and Reality* (Chapel Hill: University of North Carolina, 1963), p. 33; quoted in McGloin, p. 5.

15. The subject of Quiroga as an existentialist writer will be further developed in the following chapter.

16. "*Presente profundo*, de Elena Quiroga," *El Noticiero Universal,* August 15, 1973.

Chapter Seven

1. Pilar Merrill, *Tres motivos telúricos en la novelística de Elena Quiroga* (Ph.D. diss., University of Virginia, 1975), p. 223.

2. Quiroga mentioned this desire both in our taped interview of June 27, 1975, and in her interview with Pilar Equiza, "Elena Quiroga y la novela española de posguerra," *Mundo Hispánico,* March, 1976, p. 12.

3. This number includes *It's All Over Now, Baby Blue,* which was still in progress at the time of this writing.

4. Taped interview of June 12, 1976.

5. This characteristic of Quiroga's work is discussed in Merrill's dissertation and in Delano, "Sensory Images in the Galician Novels of Elena Quiroga."

6. Taped interview, June 27, 1975.

7. See my forthcoming article "Divorce in the Contemporary Spanish Novel," *Hispanófila.* See also Mercedes Hilda Cordero, *La novelística de Elene Quiroga: la problemática social en "Algo pasa en la calle"* (Ph. D. diss., University of Connecticut, 1976); unfortunately this dissertation came to my attention too late to be considered in the preparation of the present study.

8. I believe that Theresa Mary Hadjopoulos in her analysis of *Blood, The Sick Woman,* and *I Write Your Name* has read into Quiroga's works a feminist ideology not intended by the author. See Theresa Mary Hadjopoulos, *Four Women Novelists of Postwar Spain: Matute, Laforet, Quiroga, and Medio* (Ph.D. diss., Columbia University, 1974), pp. 87–121.

9. In our taped interview of June 12, 1976, Quiroga identified Sobejano and Francisco Ynduráin as being among the few critics who have commented on the philosophical implications of her work. Unless otherwise indicated, all opinions attributed to Quiroga are taken from that interview.

10. McGloin, p. 47.

11. Marjorie Grene. *Dreadful Freedom: A Critique of Existentialism* (Chicago: University of Chicago Press, 1948), p. 41.

12. Ernst Breisach, *Introduction to Modern Existentialism* (New York: Grove Press, 1962), p. 6.

13. Grene, p. 74.

14. Breisach, p. 5.

15. Henri Bergson, *Durée et simultanéité,* 7th ed. (Paris: Presses Universitaires de France, 1968), p. 46.

16. Ibid., p. 43.

17. Gaston Berger has suggested that "between existential time and Bergsonian duration there is only a difference of tension." See *Phénoménologie du temps et prospective* (Paris: Presses Universitaires de France, 1964), p. 206.

18. Franz G. Alexander and Sheldon T. Selesnick, *The History of Psychiatry* (New York: Harper & Row, 1966), p. 364.

19. Equiza.

Selected Bibliography

PRIMARY SOURCES

1. Novels and Novelettes

La soledad sonora. Madrid: Espasa-Calpe, 1949.

Viento del norte. Barcelona: Destino, 1951. German and French translations. In *Colección Premio Nadal,* vol. 3. Barcelona: Destino, 1970.

La sangre. Barcelona: Destino, 1952. Finnish, French, and Ukrainian translations.

Trayecto uno. Madrid: Editorial Tecnos, 1953. "La Novela del Sábado," Year I., No. 2. In *Plácida, la joven* (see below).

La otra ciudad. Madrid: Prensa Española, 1953. "La Novela del Sábado," Year I, No. 35. In *Plácida, la joven* (see below).

Algo pasa en la calle. Barcelona: Destino, 1954. German translation. In *Las mejores novelas contemporáneas,* edited by Joaquín de Entrambasaguas, vol. 12. Barcelona: Planeta, 1971.

La enferma. Barcelona: Noguer, 1955. French translation.

La careta. Barcelona: Noguer, 1955. French translation. Madrid: Ediciones del Centro, 1974. Chapter 16, in *Novelistas de 1945: Antología de LaForet, Matute y Quiroga.* Madrid: Coculsa, 1970.

Plácida, la joven y otras narraciones. Madrid: Prensa Española, 1956; Barcelona: Noguer, 1970. Includes *Plácida, la joven, Trayecto uno,* and *La otra ciudad.*

La última corrida. Barcelona: Noguer, 1958.

Tristura. Barcelona: Noguer, 1960.

Escribo tu nombre. Barcelona: Noguer, 1965. Ukrainian translation.

Presente profundo. Barcelona: Destino, 1973.

Se acabó todo, muchacha triste. Expected publication in 1977.

2. Miscellaneous and Privately Printed Works

"Prólogo" to *La condesa de Pardo Bazán sus linajes (Nobiliario),* by D. Válgoma y Díaz-Varela, Burgos, 1952. Pp. 7–14. Brief prologue to her husband's genealogical study of the important nineteenth-century writer.

"El pájaro de oro." Privately printed short story, written for family and friends.

"Carta a Cadaqués." Santander: Imprenta Bedia, 1961. Brief poetic

work, privately printed, written as a thank you for friends who
allowed her the use of their home in Cadaqués while she was at
work on a novel.
"Envió al Faramello." Madrid: Raycar, 1963. Privately printed poetic
work, including photographs, written in tribute to a family friend
in Galicia during his terminal illness.

SECONDARY SOURCES

The most complete bibliography on Quiroga and her novels, including
book reviews, appears in *Las mejores novelas contemporáneas,* edited by
Joaquín de Entrambasaguas, (Barcelona: Planeta, 1971), XII, 1305-7.

ALBORG, JUAN LUIS. *Hora actual de la novela española.* Madrid: Taurus,
1958. Pp. 191-99. Includes novels from *Viento del norte* to *La
careta.* Makes some good observations, but criticism is marred by
sexist comments and by failure to understand *La careta.*

BRENT, ALBERT. "The Novels of Elena Quiroga." *Hispania* 42 (1959),
210-13. One of the earliest studies of Quiroga's work. Discusses
her first six novels, beginning with *La soledad sonora.* Helpful introduction to the subject.

COINDREAU, MAURICE E. "Prólogo" to *La careta,* by Elena Quiroga.
Madrid: Ediciones del Centro, 1974. Pp. 9-13. Coindreau originally wrote this introduction in 1959 as the preface to his French
translation of the novel. Contains useful insights into the meaning
and style of *La careta* along with some information on Quiroga's
childhood.

CORRALES EGEA, JOSÉ. *La novela española actual (Ensayo de ordenación).* Madrid: Cuadernos para el Diálogo, 1971. Pp.
116-19, 125. Generally negative survey of novels from *Viento del
norte* through *La última corrida.* Skips *La enferma* and erroneously dates *Algo pasa en la calle* at 1960. Considers Quiroga to
be a follower, not an innovator.

CORREA CALDERÓN, E. "Galicia a través de *Viento del Norte,* de Elena
Quiroga." *Correo Literario,* May 15, 1952, p. 5. Interesting for its
defense of *Viento del norte* as a Galician novel.

DELANO, LUCILE K. "The Novelistic style of Elena Quiroga." *Kentucky
Foreign Language Quarterly* 9 (1962), 61-67. Superficial attempt
at analyzing Quiroga's stylistic devices, but to date the only article
devoted to this aspect of her work. Includes novels from *La
soledad sonora* to *Tristura.*

————. "Sensory Images in the Galician Novels of Elena Quiroga."
Kentucky Foreign Language Quarterly 10 (1963), 59-68. Somewhat more intensive analysis of one aspect of Quiroga's style. Includes a number of quotations from the novels. Emphasis on

images related to the sea and the weather.

DOMINGO, JOSÉ. "El espíritu de renovación de Elena Quiroga." In *La novela española del siglo XX*. Barcelona: Nueva Colección Labor, 1973. Vol. 2, pp. 55-56. Very brief, concise introduction to Quiroga's novels up through *Escribo tu nombre,* with emphasis on the most popular critical comments on her work. Omits the short novels and *La enferma.*

ENTRAMBASAGUAS, JOAQUÍN DE, ed. *Las mejores novelas contemporáneas.* Barcelona: Planeta, 1971. Vol. *XII, (1950-1954),* pp. 1281-307. One of the best secondary sources on Quiroga. In this introduction to his edition of *Algo pasa en la calle,* he surveys all of her work up to and including *Escribo tu nombre.* Leans heavily on his book reviews published earlier in various journals. Criticism somewhat marred by failure to identify any weak points. Contains biographical data and extensive bibliography, including numerous book reciews.

EQUIZA, PILAR. "Elena Quiroga y la novela española de posguerra." *Mundo Hispánico,* March, 1976, pp. 10-12. Interesting recent interview emphasizing the author's opinions on literature and impact of the Civil War.

FERNÁNDEZ-BRASO, MIGUEL. "Elena Quiroga. Al margen de la confusión." *Pueblo,* May 12, 1971, p. 4. Interview giving Quiroga's view of the novel, including the Latin American novel. Based partially on earlier interviews of the author.

GARCÍA PINTADO, A. "Elena Quiroga o la pasión de vivir." *ABC,* March 1, 1967, unpaginated. In spite of some factual errors, this interview of Quiroga is one of the most helpful in understanding the author's life and her ideas on the novel.

GIL, FRANCISCO. "Elena Quiroga: un mundo de silencio y esperanza." *El Alcazar,* April 27, 1973, p. 25. Interesting interview in which Quiroga talks of her parents, her view of Spain's past, and her view of the novel.

GUERRERO, OBDULIA. "Miguel Delibes y su novela *Cinco horas con Mario.*" *Cuadernos Hispanoamericanos* 70 (1967), 614-21. Includes a comparison with Quiroga's *Algo pasa en la calle.*

HADJOPOULOS, THERESA MARY. "Four Women Novelists of Postwar Spain: Matute, Laforet, Quiroga, and Medio." Ph.D. dissertation, Columbia University, 1974. Includes discussion of *La sangre, La enferma,* and *Escribo tu nombre.* Views these novels largely from a feminist perspective, very probably reading into them an ideology not intended by the author.

HOYOS, ANTONIO DE. "Elena Quiroga (El amor en dos tiempos)." In *Ocho escritores actuales.* Murcia: Aula de Cultura, 1954. Pp. 87-118. Extensive commentary on *Viento del norte* and *La sangre.*

Identifies solitude, love, and death as themes. Links her work to Galician lyricism. Includes a biographical note and conversation with the author, although the latter is not very revealing.

MAYORAL, MARINA. "Una lucha nunca acabada." *Cuadernos Hispano-americanos* 69 (1967), 553–56. Brief study of *Escribo tu nombre*. Sees the main theme of the novel as being the development of Tadea's personality and the fight for authenticity.

MCGLOIN, GENEVIÈVE G. "Elena Quiroga's *La careta:* Time and the Mask." Ph.D. dissertation, St. Louis University, 1971. General introduction to Quiroga's novels and in-depth analysis of *La careta.* In spite of a serious error in the interpretation of *La careta,* McGloin's study is an invaluable aid to the understanding of Quiroga's novelistic techniques. Useful also for discussion of stream of consciousness, time, and existentialism in relationship to the novel.

MERRILL, PILAR. "Tres motivos telúricos en la novelística de Elena Quiroga." Ph.D. dissertation, University of Virginia, 1975. Primarily a discussion of the telluric closeness between man and nature in *La soledad sonora, Viento del norte, La sangre,* and *La enferma,* but also includes commentary on various aspects of the four works.

NORA, EUGENIO G. DE. *La novela española contemporánea (1927-1960).* Madrid: Gredos, 1962. Vol. 2, pt. 2, pp. 164–71. Generally balanced criticism of novels from *La soledad sonora* through *La última corrida.* Some slight errors in biographical information and in interpretation of novels. Includes useful bibliography.

RODRÍGUEZ, PEDRO. "Elena Quiroga veinte años después." *El Siglo* (Bogotá), May 30, 1971, p. 2. Interview originally written for *Ya.* Gives background on Quiroga's family, her views on Galicia, Spain, and Spanish women.

SOBEJANO, GONZALO. *Novela española de nuestro tiempo (en busca del pueblo perdido).* Madrid: Prensa Española, 1970. Pp. 182–88. Includes Quiroga's work in his category "existential novel." Generally good introduction to her novels up through *Escribo tu nombre* except for a negative analysis of *La careta* in which he fails to perceive either Moisés' guilt or the significance of the Civil War.

TORRES RIOSECO, ARTURO. "Tres novelistas españolas." *Revista Hispánica Moderna* 31 (1965), 418–24. Generally negative criticism of novels from *Viento del norte* through *La careta,* with some positive comments on *Algo pasa en la calle.*

TRENAS, JULIO. "Así trabaja: Elena Quiroga." *Pueblo,* April 25, 1957, p. 16. Interview in which Quiroga makes specific comments on her novels and her writing habits. Identifies where she wrote each of the early novels.

URIBARRI, RAFAEL. "Elena Quiroga habla para *Diario de Navarra.*" *Diario de Navarra,* June 22, 1969, p. 27. Interview emphasizing Quiroga's view of the childhood world as a literary theme.

VÁZQUEZ DODERO, J. L. "Novela y psicología." *Nuestro Tiempo* 9 (1955), 118–21. Briefly traces Quiroga's work from *Viento del Norte* to *Algo pasa en la calle.* Considers the latter to be an excellent example of the psychological novel but has some basic errors in his understanding of the work.

VILLEGAS, JUAN. "Los motivos estructurantes de *La careta,* de Elena Quiroga." *Cuadernos Hispanoamericanos* 75 (1968), 638–48. Single most important critical study of any of Quiroga's novels. Rapidly identifies and analyzes the major stylistic, structural, and thematic tendencies of Quiroga's most difficult novel.

Index

(The works of Quiroga are listed under her name)